3 -

P9-DHD-136

BY HENRY VAN DYKE

Companionable Books
The Valley of Vision
Camp-Fires and Guide-Posts
Out-of-Doors in the Holy Land
Little Rivers
Fisherman's Luck

Days Off
The Unknown Quantity
The Ruling Passion
The Blue Flower

Poems, Collection in one volume
Songs Out of Doors

Golden Stars
The Red Flower
The Grand Canyon, and Other Poems
The White Bees, and Other Poems
The Builders, and Other Poems
Music, and Other Poems
The Toiling of Felix, and Other Poems
The House of Rimmon

Studies in Tennyson
Poems of Tennyson
Fighting for Peace

CHARLES SCRIBNER'S SONS

COMPANIONABLE BOOKS

From a photograph, copyright by Hollyer, London.

JOHN KEATS.

Painted by Joseph Severn.

COMPANIONABLE BOOKS

BY

HENRY VAN DYKE

"What is this reading, which I must learn," asked Adam, "and what is it like?"

"It is something beyond gardening," answered Raphael, "and at times you will find it a heavy task. But at its best it will be like listening through your eyes; and you shall hear the flowers laugh, the trees talk, and the stars sing."

SOLOMON SINGLEWITZ—*The Life of Adam*

NEW YORK
CHARLES SCRIBNER'S SONS
1922

Copyright, 1922, by
CHARLES SCRIBNER'S SONS

Copyright, 1920, by HARPER BROTHERS

Printed in the United States of America

Published October, 1922

To

MAXWELL STRUTHERS BURT

AUTHOR AND RANCHMAN
ONCE MY SCHOLAR
ALWAYS MY FRIEND

PREFACE

Many books are dry and dusty, there is no juice in them; and many are soon exhausted, you would no more go back to them than to a squeezed orange; but some have in them an unfailing sap, both from the tree of knowledge and from the tree of life.

By companionable books I mean those that are worth taking with you on a journey, where the weight of luggage counts, or keeping beside your bed, near the night-lamp; books that will bear reading often, and the more slowly you read them the better you enjoy them; books that not only tell you how things look and how people behave, but also interpret nature and life to you, in language of beauty and power touched with the personality of the author, so that they have a real voice audible to your spirit in the silence.

Here I have written about a few of these books which have borne me good company, in one way or another,—and about their authors, who have

PREFACE

put the best of themselves into their work. Such criticism as the volume contains is therefore mainly in the form of appreciation with reasons for it. The other kind of criticism you will find chiefly in the omissions.

So (changing the figure to suit this cabin by the sea) I send forth my new ship, hoping only that it may carry something desirable from each of the ports where it has taken on cargo, and that it may not be sunk by the enemy before it touches at a few friendly harbours.

HENRY VAN DYKE.

SYLVANORA,
Seal Harbour, Me.,
August 19, 1922.

CONTENTS

ILLUSTRATIONS

---

*In the cover design by Margaret Armstrong the books and authors
are represented by the following symbolic flowers: Bible—grapes;
Psalms—wheat; Dickens—English holly; Thackeray—English rose;
George Eliot—ivy; Keats—bleeding-heart; Wordsworth—daffodil;
Browning—pomegranate; Izaak Walton—strawberry; Johnson—
oak; Stevenson—Scottish bluebell.*

THE BOOK OF BOOKS

THE BOOK OF BOOKS

An Apologue

THERE was once an Eastern prince who was much enamoured of the art of gardening. He wished that all flowers delightful to the eye, and all fruits pleasant to the taste and good for food, should grow in his dominion, and that in growing the flowers should become more fair, the fruits more savoury and nourishing. With this thought in his mind and this desire in his heart, he found his way to the Ancient One, the Worker of Wonders who dwells in a secret place, and made known his request.

"For the care of your gardens and your orchards," said the Ancient One, "I can do nothing, since that charge has been given to you and to your people. Nor will I send blossoming plants and fruiting trees of every kind to make your kingdom rich and beautiful as by magic, lest the honour of labour should be diminished, and the slow reward of patience despised, and even the living gifts bestowed upon you

3

without toil should wither and die away. But this will I do: a single tree shall be brought to you from a far country by the hands of my servants, and you shall plant it in the midst of your land. In the body of that tree is the sap of life that was from the beginning; the leaves of it are full of healing; its flowers never fail, and its fruitage is the joy of every season. The roots of the tree shall go down to the springs of deep waters; and wherever its pollen is drifted by the wind or borne by the bees, the gardens shall put on new beauty; and wherever its seed is carried by the fowls of the air, the orchards shall yield a richer harvest. But the tree itself you shall guard and cherish and keep as I give it you, neither cutting anything away from it, nor grafting anything upon it; for the life of the tree is in all the branches, and the other trees shall be glad because of it."

As the Ancient One had spoken, so it came to pass. The land of that prince had great renown of fine flowers and delicious fruits, ever unfolding in new colours and sweeter flavours the life that was shed among them by the tree of trees.

THE BOOK OF BOOKS

I

Something like the marvel of this tale may be read in the history of the Bible. No other book in the world has had such a strange vitality, such an outgoing power of influence and inspiration. Not only has it brought to the countries in whose heart it has been set new ideals of civilization, new models of character, new conceptions of virtue and hopes of happiness; but it has also given new impulse and form to the shaping imagination of man, and begotten beauty in literature and the other arts.

Suppose, for example, that it were possible to dissolve away all the works of art which clearly owe their being to thoughts, emotions, or visions derived from the Bible,—all sculpture like Donatello's "David" and Michelangelo's "Moses"; all painting like Raphael's "Sistine Madonna" and Murillo's "Holy Family"; all music like Bach's "Passion" and Handel's "Messiah"; all poetry like Dante's "Divine Comedy" and Milton's "Paradise Lost,"— how it would impoverish the world!

The literary influence of the Bible appears the

more wonderful when we consider that it is the work of a race not otherwise potent or famous in literature. We do not know, of course, what other books may have come from the Jewish nation and vanished with whatever of power or beauty they possessed; but in those that remain there is little of exceptional force or charm for readers outside of the Hebrew race. They have no broad human appeal, no universal significance, not even any signal excellence of form and imagery. Josephus is a fairly good historian, sometimes entertaining, but not comparable to Herodotus or Thucydides or Tacitus or Gibbon. The Talmuds are vast storehouses of things new and old, where a careful searcher may now and then find a legendary gem or a quaint fragment of moral tapestry. In histories of mediæval literature, Ibn Ezra of Toledo and Rashi of Lunel are spoken of with respect. In modern letters, works as far apart as the philosophical treatises of Spinoza and the lyrics of Heinrich Heine have distinction in their kind. No one thinks that the Hebrews are lacking in great and varied talents; but how is it that in world-literature their only contribution that counts is the Bible? And how is it that it counts so immensely?

It is possible to answer by saying that in the Old Testament we have a happily made collection of the best things in the ancient literature of the Jews, and in the New Testament we have another anthology of the finest of the narratives and letters which were produced by certain writers of the same race under a new and exceedingly powerful spiritual impulse. The Bible is excellent because it contains the cream of Hebrew thought. But this answer explains nothing. It only restates the facts in another form. How did the cream rise? How did such a collection come to be made? What gives it unity and coherence underneath all its diversity? How is it that, as a clear critic has well said, "These sixty books, with all their varieties of age, authorship, literary form, are, when properly arranged, felt to draw together with a unity like the connectedness of a dramatic plot?"

There is an answer, which if it be accepted, carries with it a solution of the problem.

Suppose a race chosen by some process of selection (which need not now be discussed or defined) to develop in its strongest and most absolute form that one of man's faculties which is called the religious sense, to receive most clearly and deeply the impression of the unity, spirituality, and righteousness of a Supreme Being present in the world. Imagine that race moving through a long and varied experience under this powerful impression, now loyal to it, now rebelling against it, now misinterpreting it, now led by the voice of some prophet to understand it more fully and feel it more profoundly, but never wholly losing it for a single generation. Imagine the history of that race, its poetry, the biography of its famous men and women, the messages of its moral reformers, conceived and written in constant relation to that strongest factor of conscious life, the sense of the presence and power of the Eternal.

Suppose, now, in a time of darkness and humiliation, that there rises within that race a prophet who declares that a new era of spiritual light has come, preaches a new revelation of the Eternal, and claims in his own person to fulfil the ancient hopes and promises of a divine deliverer and redeemer. Imagine his followers, few in number, accepting his message slowly and dimly at first, guided by companionship with him into a clearer understanding and a stronger belief, until at last they are convinced that his claims are true, and that he is the saviour not only of the chosen people, but also of the whole world, the revealer of the Eternal to mankind. Imagine these disciples setting out with incredible courage to carry this message to all nations, so deeply impressed with its truth that they are supremely happy to suffer and die for it, so filled with the passion of its meaning that they dare attempt to remodel the life of the world with it. Suppose a human story like this underneath the writing of the books which are gathered in the Bible, and you have an explanation—it seems to me the only reasonable explanation—of their surpassing quality and their strange unity.

This story is not a mere supposition: its general outline, stated in these terms, belongs to the realm of facts which cannot reasonably be questioned. What more is needed to account for the story itself, what potent and irresistible reality is involved in this record of experience, I do not now ask. This is not an estimate of the religious authority of the Bible, nor of its inspiration in the theological sense of that word, but only of something less important, though no less real—its literary influence.

II

The fountain-head of the power of the Bible in literature lies in its nearness to the very springs and sources of human life—life taken seriously, earnestly, intensely; life in its broadest meaning, including the inward as well as the outward; life interpreted in its relation to universal laws and eternal values. It is this vital quality in the narratives, the poems, the allegories, the meditations, the discourses, the letters, gathered in this book, that gives it first place among the books of the world not only for currency, but also for greatness.

For the currency of literature depends in the long run upon the breadth and vividness of its human appeal. And the greatness of literature depends upon the intensive significance of those portions of

life which it depicts and interprets. Now, there is
no other book which reflects so many sides and
aspects of human experience as the Bible, and this
fact alone would suffice to give it a world-wide interest and make it popular. But it mirrors them
all, whether they belong to the chronicles of kings
and conquerors, or to the obscure records of the
lowliest of labourers and sufferers, in the light of a
conviction that they are all related to the will and
purpose of the Eternal. This illuminates every figure with a divine distinction, and raises every event
to the nth power of meaning. It is this fact that
gives the Bible its extraordinary force as literature
and makes it great.

*Born in the East and clothed in Oriental form and
imagery, the Bible walks the ways of all the world with
familiar feet and enters land after land to find its own
everywhere. It has learned to speak in hundreds of
languages to the heart of man. It comes into the palace to tell the monarch that he is a servant of the Most
High, and into the cottage to assure the peasant that
he is a son of God. Children listen to its stories with
wonder and delight, and wise men ponder them as*

11

parables of life. It has a word of peace for the time of peril, a word of comfort for the day of calamity, a word of light for the hour of darkness. Its oracles are repeated in the assembly of the people, and its counsels whispered in the ear of the lonely. The wicked and the proud tremble at its warning, but to the wounded and the penitent it has a mother's voice. The wilderness and the solitary place have been made glad by it, and the fire on the hearth has lit the reading of its well-worn page. It has woven itself into our deepest affections and coloured our dearest dreams; so that love and friendship, sympathy and devotion, memory and hope, put on the beautiful garments of its treasured speech, breathing of frankincense and myrrh.

Above the cradle and beside the grave its great words come to us uncalled. They fill our prayers with power larger than we know, and the beauty of them lingers on our ear long after the sermons which they adorned have been forgotten. They return to us swiftly and quietly, like doves flying from far away. They surprise us with new meanings, like springs of water breaking forth from the mountain beside a long-trodden path. They grow richer, as pearls do when they are worn near the heart.

THE BOOK OF BOOKS

No man is poor or desolate who has this treasure for his own. When the landscape darkens and the trembling pilgrim comes to the Valley named of the Shadow, he is not afraid to enter: he takes the rod and staff of Scripture in his hand; he says to friend and comrade, "Good-by; we shall meet again"; and comforted by that support, he goes toward the lonely pass as one who walks through darkness into light.

It would be strange indeed if a book which has played such a part in human life had not exercised an extraordinary influence upon literature. As a matter of fact, the Bible has called into existence tens of thousands of other books devoted to the exposition of its meaning, the defense and illustration of its doctrine, the application of its teaching, or the record of its history. The learned Fabricius, in the early part of the eighteenth century, published a *catalogue raisonné* of such books, filling seven hundred quarto pages.* Since that time the length of the list has probably more than trebled. In addition, we must reckon the many books of hostile criticism and contrary argument which the Bible has evoked, and which are an evidence of

* *Syllabus Scriptorum Veterum Recentiumque qui Veritatem Religionis Christianæ Asseruerunt:* Hamburg, 1725.

revolt against the might of its influence. All this tangle of Biblical literature has grown up around it like a vast wood full of all manner of trees, great and small, useful and worthless, fruit-trees, timber-trees, berry-bushes, briers, and poison-vines. But all of them, even the most beautiful and tall, look like undergrowth, when we compare them with the mighty oak of Scripture, towering in perennial grandeur, the father of the forest.

Among the patristic writers there were some of great genius like Origen and Chrysostom and Augustine. The mediæval schools of theology produced men of philosophic power, like Anselm and Thomas Aquinas; of spiritual insight, like the author of the *Imitatio Christi*. The eloquence of France reached its height in the discourses of Bossuet, Bourdaloue, and Massillon. German became one of the potent tongues of literature when Martin Luther used it in his tracts and sermons, and Herder's *Geist der hebräischen Poesie* is one of the great books in criticism. In English, to mention such names as Hooker and Fuller and Jeremy Taylor is to recall the dignity, force, and splendour of prose at its best.

Yet none of these authors has produced anything to rival the book from which they drew their common inspiration.

In the other camp, though there have been many brilliant assailants, not one has surpassed, or even equalled, in the estimation of the world, the literary excellence of the book which they attacked. The mordant wit of Voltaire, the lucid and melancholy charm of Renan, have not availed to drive or draw the world away from the Bible; and the effect of all assaults has been to leave it more widely read, better understood, and more intelligently admired than ever before.

Now it must be admitted that the same thing is true, at least in some degree, of other books which are held to be sacred or quasi-sacred: they are superior to the distinctively theological literature which has grown up about them. I suppose nothing of the Mussulmans is as great as the "Koran," nothing of the Hindus as great as the "Vedas"; and though the effect of the Confucian classics, from the literary point of view, may not have been altogether good, their supremacy in the religious library of the Chinese is unquestioned. But the singular and noteworthy thing about the influence of the Bible is the extent to which it has permeated general literature, the mark which it has made in all forms of belles-lettres. To treat this subject adequately one would need to write volumes. In this chapter I can touch but briefly on a few points of the outline as they come out in English literature.

III

In the Old-English period, the predominant influence of the Scriptures may be seen in the frequency with which the men of letters turned to them for subjects, and in the Biblical colouring and texture of thought and style. Cædmon's famous "Hymn" and the other poems like "Genesis," "Exodus," "Daniel," and "Judith," which were once ascribed to him; Cynewulf's "Crist," "The Fates of the Apostles," "The Dream of the Rood"; Ælfric's "Homilies" and his paraphrases of certain books of Scripture—these early fruits of our literature are all the offspring of the Bible.

In the Middle-English period, that anonymous

masterpiece "Pearl" is full of the spirit of Christian mysticism, and the two poems called "Cleanness" and "Patience," probably written by the same hand, are free and spirited versions of stories from the Bible. "The Vision of Piers the Plowman," formerly ascribed to William Langland, but now supposed by some scholars to be the work of four or five different authors, was the most popular poem of the latter half of the fourteenth century. It is a vivid picture of the wrongs and sufferings of the labouring man, a passionate satire on the corruptions of the age in church and state, an eloquent appeal for a return to truth and simplicity. The feeling and the imagery of Scripture pervade it with a strange power and charm; in its reverence for poverty and toil it leans closely and confidently upon the example of Jesus; and at the end it makes its ploughman hero appear in some mystic way as a type, first of the crucified Saviour, and then of the church which is the body of Christ.

It was about this time, the end of the fourteenth century, that John Wyclif and his disciples, feeling the need of the support of the Bible in their work as reformers, took up and completed the task of translating it entirely into the English tongue of the common people. This rude but vigourous version was revised and improved by John Purvey. It rested mainly upon the Latin version of St. Jerome. At the beginning of the sixteenth century William Tindale made an independent translation of the New Testament from the original Greek, a virile and enduring piece of work, marked by strength and simplicity, and setting a standard for subsequent English translations. Coverdale's version of the Scriptures was published in 1535, and was announced as made "out of Douche and Latyn"; that is to say, it was based upon the German of Luther and the Zurich Bible, and upon the Vulgate of St. Jerome; but it owed much to Tindale, to whose manly force it added a certain music of diction and grace of phrase which may still be noted in the Psalms as they are rendered in the Anglican Prayer-Book. Another translation, marked by accurate scholarship, was made by English Puritans at Geneva, and still another, characterized by a richer Latinized style, was made by English Catholics living in exile at Rheims, and was known as "the Douai Version," from the fact that it was first published in its complete form in that city in 1609–1610.

Meantime, in 1604, a company of scholars had been appointed by King James I in England to make a new translation "out of the original tongues, and with the former translations diligently compared and revised." These forty-seven men had the advantage of all the work of their predecessors, the benefit of all the discussion over doubtful words and phrases, and the "unearned increment" of riches which had come into the English language since the days of Wyclif. The result of their labours, published in 1611, was the so-called "Authorized Version," a monument of English prose in its prime: clear, strong, direct, yet full of subtle rhythms and strange colours; now moving as simply as a shepherd's song, in the Twenty-third Psalm; now marching with majestic harmonies, in the book of Job; now reflecting the lowliest forms of human life, in the Gospel stories; and now flashing with celestial splendours in the visions of the Apocalypse;

vivid without effort; picturesque without exaggeration; sinewy without strain; capable alike of the deepest tenderness and the most sublime majesty; using a vocabulary of only six thousand words to build a book which, as Macaulay said, "if everything else in our language should perish, would alone suffice to show the whole extent of its beauty and power."

The literary excellence of this version, no doubt, did much to increase the influence of the Bible in literature and confirm its place as the central book in the life of those who speak and write the English tongue. Consider a few of the ways in which this influence may be traced.

IV

First of all, it has had a general effect upon English writing, helping to preserve it from the opposite faults of vulgarity and affectation. Coleridge long ago remarked upon the tendency of a close study of the Bible to elevate a writer's style. There is a certain naturalness, inevitableness, propriety of form to substance, in the language of Scripture which communicates to its readers a feeling for the fitness of words; and this in itself is the first requisite of good writing. Sincerity is the best part of dignity.

The English of our Bible is singularly free from the vice of preciosity: it is not far-sought, overnice, elaborate. Its plainness is a rebuking contrast to all forms of euphuism. It does not encourage a direct imitation of itself; for the comparison between the original and the copy makes the latter look pale and dull. Even in the age which produced the authorized version, its style was distinct and remarkable. As Hallam has observed, it was "not the English of Daniel, of Raleigh, or Bacon." It was something larger, at once more ancient and more modern, and therefore well fitted to become not an invariable model, but an enduring standard. Its words come to it from all sources; they are not chosen according to the foolish theory that a word of Anglo-Saxon origin is always stronger and simpler than a Latin derivative. Take the beginning of the Forty-sixth Psalm:

"God is our refuge and strength, a very present

help in trouble. Therefore will not we fear, though the earth be removed, and though the mountains be carried into the midst of the sea; though the waters thereof roar and be troubled, though the mountains shake with the swelling thereof."

Or take this passage from the Epistle to the Romans:

"Be kindly affectioned one to another with brotherly love; in honour preferring one another; not slothful in business; fervent in spirit; serving the Lord; rejoicing in hope; patient in tribulation; continuing instant in prayer; distributing to the necessity of saints; given to hospitality."

Here is a style that adapts itself by instinct to its subject, and whether it uses Saxon words like "strength" and "help" and "love" and "hope," or Latin words like "refuge" and "trouble" and "present" and "fervent" and "patient" and "prayer" and "hospitality," weaves them into a garment worthy of the thought.

The literary influence of a great, popular book written in such a style is both inspiring and conservative. It survives the passing modes of prose in each generation, and keeps the present in touch with the past. It preserves a sense of balance and proportion in a language whose perils lie in its liberties and in the indiscriminate use of its growing wealth. And finally it keeps a medium of communication open between the learned and the simple; for the two places where the effect of the Bible upon the English language may be most clearly felt are in the natural speech of the plain people and in the finest passages of great authors.

V

Following this line of the influence of the Bible upon language as the medium of literature, we find, in the next place, that it has contributed to our common speech a great number of phrases which are current everywhere. Sometimes these phrases are used in a merely conventional way. They serve as counters in a long extemporaneous prayer, or as padding to a page of dull and pious prose. But at other times they illuminate the sentence with a new radiance; they clarify its meaning with a true symbol; they enhance its value with rich associations;

they are "sweeter than honey and the honey-comb."

Take for example such phrases as these: "a good old age," "the wife of thy bosom," "the apple of his eye," "gathered to his fathers," "a mother in Israel," "a land flowing with milk and honey," "the windows of heaven," "the fountains of the great deep," "living fountains of waters," "the valley of decision," "cometh up as a flower," "a garden enclosed," "one little ewe lamb," "thou art the man," "a still, small voice," "as the sparks fly upward," "swifter than a weaver's shuttle," "miserable comforters," "the strife of tongues," "the tents of Kedar," "the cry of the humble," "the lofty looks of man," "the pride of life," "from strength to strength," "as a dream when one awaketh," "the wings of the morning," "stolen waters," "a dinner of herbs," "apples of gold in pictures of silver," "better than rubies," "a lion in the way," "vanity of vanities," "no discharge in that war," "the little foxes that spoil the vines," "terrible as an army with banners," "precept upon precept, line upon line," "as a drop of a bucket," "whose merchants are princes," "trodden the wine-press alone," "the rose of Sharon and the lily of the valley," "the highways and hedges," "the salt of the earth," "the burden and heat of the day," "the signs of the times," "a pearl of great price," "what God hath joined together," "the children of light," "the powers that be," "if the trumpet give an uncertain sound," "the fashion of this world," "decently and in order," "a thorn in the flesh," "labour of love," "a cloud of witnesses," "to entertain angels unawares," "faithful unto death," "a crown of life." Consider also those expressions which carry with them distinctly the memory of some ancient story: "the fleshpots of Egypt," "manna in the wilderness," "a mess of pottage," "Joseph's coat," "the driving of Jehu," "the mantle of Elijah," "the widow's mite," "the elder brother," "the kiss of Judas," "the house of Martha," "a friend of publicans and sinners," "many mansions," "bearing the cross." Into such phrases as these, which are familiar to us all, the Bible has poured a wealth of meaning far beyond the measure of the bare words. They call up visions and reveal mysteries.

VI

Direct, but not always accurate, quotations from Scripture and allusions to Biblical characters and events are very numerous in English literature. They are found in all sorts of books. Professor Albert T. Cook has recently counted sixty-three in a volume of descriptive sketches of Italy, twelve in a book on wild animals, and eighteen in a novel by Thomas Hardy. A special study of the Biblical references in Tennyson has been made,* and more than five hundred of them have been found.

Bishop Charles Wordsworth has written a book on *Shakespeare's Knowledge and Use of the Bible,*† and shown "how fully and how accurately the general tenor of the facts recorded in the sacred narrative was present to his mind," and "how Scriptural are the conceptions which Shakespeare had of the being and attributes of God, of His general and particular Providence, of His revelation to man, of

---

* *The Poetry of Tennyson.* Scribner's: New York, 1889–1920.
† Smith, Elder & Co.: London, 1880.

our duty toward Him and toward each other, of
human life and of human death, of time and of
eternity." It is possible that the bishop benevo-
lently credits the dramatist with a more invariable
and complete orthodoxy than he possessed. But
certainly Shakespeare knew the Bible well, and felt
the dramatic value of allusions and illustrations
which were sure to be instantly understood by the
plain people. It is his Antonio, in *The Merchant
of Venice*, who remarks that "the Devil can cite
Scripture for his purpose," evidently referring to the
Gospel story of the evil one who tried to tempt
Jesus with a verse from the Psalms.

The references to the Bible in the poetry of
Robert Browning have been very carefully exam-
ined by Mrs. Machen in an admirable little book.*
It is not too much to say that his work is crowded
with Scriptural quotations, allusions, and imagery.
He follows Antonio's maxim, and makes his bad
characters, like Bishop Blougram and Sludge the
Medium, cite from Holy Writ to cloak their hypocrisy or excuse their villainy. In his longest

* *The Bible in Browning.* Macmillan: New York, 1903.

poem, *The Ring and the Book*, there are said to be more than five hundred Biblical references.

But more remarkable even than the extent to which this material drawn from the Scriptures has been used by English writers, is the striking effect which it produces when it is well used. With what pathos does Sir Walter Scott, in *The Heart of Midlothian*, make old Davie Deans bow his head when he sees his daughter Effie on trial for her life, and mutter to himself, "Ichabod! my glory is departed!" How magnificently does Ruskin enrich his *Sesame and Lilies* with that passage from Isaiah in which the fallen kings of Hades start from their thrones to greet the newly fallen with the cry, "Art thou also become weak as we? Art thou become like unto us?" How grandly do the images and thoughts of the last chapters of Deuteronomy roll through Kipling's *Recessional*, with its Scriptural refrain, "Lest we forget!"

There are some works of literature in English since the sixteenth century which are altogether Biblical in subject and colouring. Chief among these in prose is *The Pilgrim's Progress* of John Bunyan, and in verse, the *Paradise Lost, Paradise Regained,* and *Samson Agonistes* of John Milton. These are already classics. Some day a place near them will be given to Browning's *Saul* and *A Death in the Desert;* but for that we must wait until their form has stood the test of time.

In general it may be observed—and the remark holds good of the works just mentioned—that a Scriptural story or poem is most likely to succeed when it takes its theme, directly or by suggestion, from the Bible, and carries it into a region of imagination, a border-realm, where the author is free to work without paraphrase or comparison with the sacred writers. It is for this reason that both *Samson Agonistes* and *Paradise Lost* are superior to *Paradise Regained.*

VII

The largest and most important influence of the Bible in literature lies beyond all these visible effects upon language and style and imagery and form. It comes from the strange power of the book to nourish and inspire, to mould and guide, the inner life of man. "*It finds me*," said Coleridge; and the word of the philosopher is one that the plain man can understand and repeat.

The hunger for happiness which lies in every human heart can never be satisfied without righteousness; and the reason why the Bible reaches down so deep into the breast of man is because it brings news of a kingdom which *is* righteousness and peace and joy in the Holy Spirit. It brings this news not in the form of a dogma, a definition, a scientific statement, but in the form of literature, a living picture of experience, a perfect ideal embodied in a Character and a Life. And because it does this, it has inspiration for those who write in the service of truth and humanity.

The Bible has been the favourite book of those who were troubled and downtrodden, and of those who bore the great burden of a great task. New light has broken forth from it to lead the upward struggle of mankind from age to age. Men have come back to it because they could not do without it. Nor will its influence wane, its radiance be darkened, unless literature ceases to express the noblest of human longings, the highest of human hopes, and mankind forgets all that is now incarnate in the central figure of the Bible,—the Divine Deliverer.

POETRY IN THE PSALMS

POETRY IN THE PSALMS

THERE are three ways in which we may read the Bible.

We may come to it as the divinely inspired rule of faith and conduct. This is the point of view from which it appears most precious to religion. It gives us the word of God to teach us what to believe and how to live.

We may consider it as a collection of historical books, written under certain conditions, and reflecting, in their contents and in their language, the circumstances in which they were produced. This is the aspect in which criticism regards the Bible; and its intellectual interest, as well as its religious value, is greatly enhanced by a clear vision of the truth about it from this point of view.

We may study it also as literature. We may see in it a noble and impassioned interpretation of nature and life, uttered in language of beauty and sublimity, touched with the vivid colours of human personality, and embodied in forms of enduring literary art.

None of these three ways of studying the Bible is hostile to the others. On the contrary, they are helpful to one another, because each of them gives us knowledge of a real factor in the marvellous influence of the Bible in the world.

The true lover of the Bible has an interest in all the elements of its life as an immortal book. He wishes to discern, and rightly to appreciate, the method of its history, the spirit of its philosophy, the significance of its fiction, the power of its eloquence, and the charm of its poetry. He wishes this all the more because he finds in it something which is not in any other book: a vision of God, a hope for man, and an inspiration to righteousness which seem to him divine. As the worshipper in the Temple would observe the art and structure of the carven beams of cedar and the lily-work on the tops of the pillars the more attentively because they beautified the house of his God, so the man who has a religious faith in the Bible will study more eagerly and carefully the literary forms of the book in which the Holy Spirit speaks forever.

It is in this spirit that I wish to consider the poetical element in the Psalms. The comfort, help, and guidance that they bring to our spiritual life will not be diminished, but increased, by a perception of their exquisite form and finish. If a king sent a golden cup full of cheering cordial to a weary man, he might well admire the two-fold bounty of the royal gift. The beauty of the vessel would make the draught more grateful and refreshing. And if the cup were inexhaustible, if it filled itself anew as often as it touched the lips, then the very shape and adornment of it would become significant and precious. It would be an inestimable possession, a singing goblet, a treasure of life.

John Milton, whose faith in religion was as exalted as his mastery of the art of poetry was perfect, has expressed in a single sentence the spirit in which I would approach the poetic study of the Book of Psalms: "Not in their divine arguments alone, but in the very critical art of composition, the Psalms may be easily made to appear over all kinds of lyric poetry incomparable."

I

Let us remember at the outset that a considerable part of the value of the Psalms as poetry will lie beyond our reach. We cannot precisely measure it, nor give it full appreciation, simply because we are dealing with the Psalms only as we have them in our English Bible. This is a real drawback; and it is well to understand clearly the two things that we lose in reading the Psalms in this way.

First, we lose the beauty and the charm of verse. This is a serious loss. Poetry and verse are not the same thing, but they are so intimately related that it is difficult to divide them. Indeed, according to certain definitions of poetry, it would seem almost impossible.

Yet who will deny that the Psalms as we have them in the English Bible are really and truly poetical?

The only way out of this difficulty that I can see is to distinguish between verse as the formal element and imaginative emotion as the essential element in poetry. In the original production of a poem, it seems to me, it is just to say that the embodiment in metrical language is a law of art which must be observed. But in the translation of a poem (which is a kind of reflection of it in a mirror) the verse may be lost without altogether losing the spirit of the poem.

Take an illustration from another art. A statue has the symmetry of solid form. You can look at it from all sides, and from every side you can see the balance and rhythm of the parts. In a photograph this solidity of form disappears. You see only a flat surface. But you still recognize it as the reflection of a statue.

The Psalms were undoubtedly written, in the original Hebrew, according to a system of versification, and perhaps to some extent with forms of rhyme.

The older scholars, like Lowth and Herder, held that such a system existed, but could not be recovered. Later scholars, like Ewald, evolved a system of their own. Modern scholarship, represented by such authors as Professors Cheyne and Briggs, is reconstructing and explaining more accurately the

39

Hebrew versification. But, for the present at least, the only thing that is clear is that this system must remain obscure to us. It cannot be reproduced in English. The metrical versions of the Psalms are the least satisfactory. The poet Cowley said of them, "They are so far from doing justice to David that methinks they revile him worse than Shimei."* We must learn to appreciate the poetry in the Psalms without the aid of those symmetries of form and sound in which they first appeared. This is a serious loss. Poetry without verse is like a bride without a bridal garment.

The second thing that we lose in reading the Psalms in English is something even more important. It is the heavy tax on the wealth of its meaning, which all poetry must pay when it is imported from one country to another, through the medium of translation.

The most subtle charm of poetry is its suggestiveness; and much of this comes from the magical power which words acquire over memory and imagination, from their associations. This intimate and

* "The Works of Mr. Abraham Cowley." London, 1710. Preface to *Pindarique Odes*, volume I, page 184.

personal charm must be left behind when a poem passes from one language to another. The accompaniment, the harmony of things remembered and beloved, which the very words of the song once awakened, is silent now. Nothing remains but the naked melody of thought. If this is pure and strong, it will gather new associations; as, indeed, the Psalms have already done in English, so that their familiar expressions have become charged with musical potency. And yet I suppose such phrases as "a tree planted by the rivers of water," "a fruitful vine in the innermost parts of the house," "the mountains round about Jerusalem," can never bring to us the full sense of beauty, the enlargement of heart, that they gave to the ancient Hebrews. But, in spite of this double loss, in the passage from verse to prose and from Hebrew to English, the poetry in the Psalms is so real and vital and imperishable that every reader feels its beauty and power.

It retains one valuable element of poetic form. This is that balancing of the parts of a sentence, one against another, to which Bishop Lowth first gave the familiar name of "parallelism."* The effect of

* Lowth, *De Sacra Poesi Hebræorum Praelectiones.* Oxon., 1753.

41

this simple artifice, learned from Nature herself, is singularly pleasant and powerful. It is the rise and fall of the fountain, the ebb and flow of the tide, the tone and overtone of the chiming bell. The two-fold utterance seems to bear the thought onward like the wings of a bird. A German writer compares it very exquisitely to "the heaving and sinking of the troubled heart."

It is this "parallelism" which gives such a familiar charm to the language of the Psalms. Unconsciously, and without recognizing the nature of the attraction, we grow used to the double cadence, the sound and the echo, and learn to look for its recurrence with delight.

O come let us sing unto the Lord;
Let us make a joyful noise to the rock of our salvation,
Let us come before his presence with thanksgiving;
And make a joyful noise unto him with psalms.

If we should want a plain English name for this method of composition we might call it *thought-rhyme*. It is easy to find varied illustrations of its beauty and of its power to emphasize large and simple ideas.

Take for instance that very perfect psalm with which the book begins—a poem so complete, so compact, so delicately wrought that it seems like a sonnet. The subject is *The Two Paths.*

The first part describes the way of the good man. It has three divisions.

The first verse gives a description of his conduct by negatives—telling us what he does not do. There is a triple thought-rhyme here.

Blessed is the man that walketh not in the counsel of
    the ungodly,
Nor standeth in the way of sinners,
Nor sitteth in the seat of the scornful.

The second verse describes his character positively, with a double thought-rhyme.

But his delight is in the law of the Lord;
And in his law doth he meditate day and night.

The third verse tells us the result of this character and conduct, in a fourfold thought-rhyme.

He shall be like a tree planted by the rivers of water:
That bringeth forth his fruit in his season:
His leaf also shall not wither:
And whatsoever he doeth shall prosper.

43

The second part of the psalm describes the way of the evil man. In the fourth verse there is a double thought-rhyme.

> The ungodly are not so:
> But are like the chaff which the wind driveth away.

In the fifth verse the consequences of this worthless, fruitless, unrooted life are shown, again with a double cadence of thought, the first referring to the judgment of God, the second to the judgment of men.

Therefore the ungodly shall not stand in the judgment:
Nor sinners in the congregation of the righteous.

The third part of the psalm is a terse, powerful couplet, giving the reason for the different ending of the two paths.

> For the Lord knoweth the way of the righteous:
> But the way of the ungodly shall perish.

The thought-rhyme here is one of contrast.

A poem of very different character from this brief, serious, impersonal sonnet is found in the Forty-sixth Psalm, which might be called a National

Anthem. Here again the poem is divided into three parts.

The first part (verses first to third) expresses a sense of joyful confidence in the Eternal, amid the tempests and confusions of earth. The thought-rhymes are in couplets; and the second phrase, in each case, emphasizes and enlarges the idea of the first phrase.

> God is our refuge and strength:
> A very present help in trouble.

The second part (verses fourth to seventh) describes the peace and security of the city of God, surrounded by furious enemies, but rejoicing in the Eternal Presence. The parallel phrases here follow the same rule as in the first part. The concluding phrase is the stronger, the more emphatic. The seventh verse gives the refrain or chorus of the anthem.

> The Lord of hosts is with us:
> The God of Jacob is our refuge.

The last part (verses eighth to tenth) describes in a very vivid and concrete way the deliverance of the people that have trusted in the Eternal. It begins with a couplet, like those which have gone before. Then follow two stanzas of triple thought-rhymes, in which the thought is stated and intensified with each repetition.

> He maketh wars to cease unto the end of the earth:
> He breaketh the bow, and cutteth the spear in sunder:
> He burneth the chariot in the fire.
>
> Be still, and know that I am God:
> I will be exalted among the heathen:
> I will be exalted in the earth.

The anthem ends with a repetition of the refrain.

A careful study of the Psalms, even in English, will enable the thoughtful reader to derive new pleasure from them, by tracing the many modes and manners in which this poetic form of thought-rhyme is used to bind the composition together, and to give balance and harmony to the poem.

Another element of poetic form can be discerned in the Psalms, not directly, in the English version, but by its effects. I mean the curious artifice of alphabetic arrangement. It was a favourite practice among Hebrew poets to begin their verses with the successive letters of the alphabet, or sometimes to vary the device by making every verse in a strophe begin with one letter, and every verse in the next strophe with the following letter, and so on to the end. The Twenty-fifth and the Thirty-seventh Psalms were written by the first of these rules; the One Hundred and Nineteenth Psalm follows the second plan.

Of course the alphabetic artifice disappears entirely in the English translation. But its effects remain. The Psalms written in this manner usually have but a single theme, which is repeated over and over again, in different words and with new illustrations. They are kaleidoscopic. The material does not change, but it is turned this way and that way, and shows itself in new shapes and arrangements. These alphabetic psalms are characterized by poverty of action and richness of expression.

II

Milton has already reminded us that the Psalms belong to the second of the three orders into which the Greeks, with clear discernment, divided all poetry: the epic, the lyric, and the dramatic. The Psalms are rightly called lyrics because they are chiefly concerned with the immediate and imaginative expression of real feeling. It is the personal and emotional note that predominates. They are inward, confessional, intense; outpourings of the quickened spirit; self-revelations of the heart. It is for this reason that we should never separate them in our thought from the actual human life out of which they sprung. We must feel the warm pulse of humanity in them in order to comprehend their meaning and immortal worth. So far as we can connect them with the actual experience of men, this will help us to appreciate their reality and power. The effort to do this will make plain to us some other things which it is important to remember.

We shall see at once that the book does not come from a single writer, but from many authors and ages. It represents the heart of man in communion with God through a thousand years of history, from Moses to Nehemiah, perhaps even to the time of the Maccabean revival. It is, therefore, something very much larger and better than an individual book.

It is the golden treasury of lyrics gathered from the life of the Hebrew people, the hymn-book of the Jews. And this gives to it a singular and precious quality of brotherhood. The fault, or at least the danger, of modern lyrical poetry is that it is too solitary and separate in its tone. It tends towards exclusiveness, over-refinement, morbid sentiment. Many Christian hymns suffer from this defect. But the Psalms breathe a spirit of human fellowship even when they are most intensely personal. The poet rejoices or mourns in solitude, it may be, but he is not alone in spirit. He is one of the people. He is conscious always of the ties that bind him to his brother men. Compare the intense selfishness of the modern hymn:

> I can but perish if I go;
> I am resolved to try;
> For if I stay away, I know
> I shall forever die;

with the generous penitence of the Fifty-first Psalm:

> Then will I teach transgressors thy way;
> And sinners shall be converted unto thee.

It is important to observe that there are several different kinds of lyrics among the Psalms. Some of them are simple and natural outpourings of a single feeling, like *A Shepherd's Song about His Shepherd*, the incomparable Twenty-third Psalm.

This little poem is a perfect melody. It would be impossible to express a pure, unmixed emotion—the feeling of joy in the Divine Goodness—more simply, with a more penetrating lyrical charm. The "valley of the death-shadow," the "enemies" in whose presence the table is spread, are but dimly suggested in the background. The atmosphere of the psalm is clear and bright. The singing shepherd walks in light. The whole world is the House of the Lord, and life is altogether gladness.

How different is the tone, the quality, of the One Hundred and Nineteenth Psalm! This is not a melody, but a harmony; not a song, but an ode. The ode has been defined as "a strain of exalted and enthusiastic lyrical verse, directed to a fixed purpose and dealing progressively with one dignified theme." * This definition precisely fits the One Hundred and Nineteenth Psalm.

* *English Odes*, selected by Edmund Gosse. Preface, page xiii.

POETRY IN THE PSALMS

Its theme is *The Eternal Word*. Every verse in the poem, except one, contains some name or description of the law, commandments, testimonies, precepts, statutes, or judgments of Jehovah. Its enthusiasm for the Divine Righteousness never fails from beginning to end. Its fixed purpose is to kindle in other hearts the flame of devotion to the one Holy Law. It closes with a touch of magnificent pathos—a confession of personal failure and an assertion of spiritual loyalty:

> I have gone astray like a lost sheep:
> Seek thy servant:
> For I do not forget thy commandments.

The Fifteenth Psalm I should call a short didactic lyric. Its title is *The Good Citizen*. It begins with a question:

> Lord, who shall abide in thy tabernacle?
> Who shall dwell in thy holy hill?

This question is answered by the description of a man whose character corresponds to the law of God. First there is a positive sketch in three broad lines:

> He that walketh uprightly,
> And worketh righteousness,
> And speaketh truth in his heart.

51

Then comes a negative characterization in a finely touched triplet:

> He that backbiteth not with his tongue,
> Nor doeth evil to his neighbor,
> Nor taketh up a reproach against his neighbor.

This is followed by a couplet containing a strong contrast:

> In whose eyes a vile person is contemned:
> But he honoureth them that fear the Lord.

Then the description goes back to the negative style again and three more touches are added to the picture:

> He that sweareth to his own hurt and changeth not,
> He that putteth not out his money to usury,
> Nor taketh reward against the innocent.

The poem closes with a single vigourous line, summing up the character of the good citizen and answering the question of the first verse with a new emphasis of security and permanence:

> He that doeth these things shall never be moved.

The Seventy-eighth, One Hundred and Fifth, and One Hundred and Sixth Psalms are lyrical ballads. They tell the story of Israel in Egypt, and in the Wilderness, and in Canaan, with swift, stirring phrases, and with splendid flashes of imagery. Take this passage from the Seventy-eighth Psalm as an example:

He clave the rocks in the wilderness,
And gave them drink out of the great depths.

He brought streams also out of the rock,
And caused waters to run down like rivers.

And they sinned yet more against him,
Provoking the Most High in the wilderness.

They tempted God in their hearts,
Asking meat for their lust.

Yea, they spake against God:
They said, *Can God furnish a table in the wilderness?*

Behold, he smote the rock that the waters gushed out,
And the streams overflowed;

Can he give bread also?
Can he provide flesh for his people?

Therefore the Lord heard and was wroth:
So a fire was kindled against Jacob,
And anger also came up against Israel:
Because they believed not in God,
And trusted not in his salvation:

Though he had commanded the clouds from above,
And opened the doors of heaven,
And had rained down manna upon them to eat,
And had given them of the corn of heaven,
Man did eat angel's food:

He sent them meat to the full.
He caused an east wind to blow in the heaven,
And by his power he brought in the south wind.
He rained flesh also upon them as dust,
And feathered fowls like as the sand of the sea.

And he let it fall in the midst of their camp,
Round about their habitations;
So they did eat and were filled,
For he gave them their own desire.

They were not estranged from their lust:
But while the meat was yet in their mouths,
The wrath of God came upon them, and slew the fattest of
    them,
And smote down the chosen men of Israel.

The Forty-fifth Psalm is a Marriage Ode: the
Hebrew title calls it a Love Song. It bears all the
marks of having been composed for some royal
wedding-feast in Jerusalem.

There are many nature lyrics among the Psalms.
The Twenty-ninth is notable for its rugged realism.
It is a Song of Thunder.

> The voice of the Lord breaketh the cedars:
> Yea, the Lord breaketh the cedars of Lebanon:
> He maketh them also to skip like a calf:
> Lebanon and Sirion like a young unicorn.

The One Hundred and Fourth, on the contrary, is full of calm sublimity and meditative grandeur.

> O, Lord, my God, thou art very great:
> Thou art clothed with honour and majesty:
>
> Who coverest thyself with light as with a garment;
> Who stretchest out the heavens like a curtain.

The Nineteenth is famous for its splendid comparison between "the starry heavens and the moral law."

I think that we may find also some dramatic lyrics among the Psalms—poems composed to express the feelings of an historic person, like David or Solomon, in certain well-known and striking experiences of his life. That a later writer should thus embody and express the truth dramatically through the personality of some great hero of the past, involves no falsehood. It is a mode of utterance which has been common to the literature of all lands and of all ages. Such a method of composition would certainly be no hindrance to the spirit of inspiration. The Thirty-first Psalm, for instance, is ascribed by the title to David. But there is strong reason, in the phraseology and in the spirit of the poem, to believe that it was written by the Prophet Jeremiah.

III

It is not to be supposed that our reverence for the Psalms in their moral and religious aspects will make us put them all on the same level poetically. There is a difference among the books of the New Testament in regard to the purity and dignity of the Greek in which they are written. There is a difference among St. Paul's Epistles in regard to the clearness and force of their style. There is a difference even among the chapters of the same epistle in regard to the beauty of thought and language. In the First Epistle to the Corinthians, the thirteenth chapter is poetic, and the fourteenth is prosaic. Why should there not be a difference in poetic quality among the Psalms?

There is a difference. The honest reader will recognize it. It will be no harm to him if he should have his favourites among the poems which have been gathered from many centuries into this great collection.

There are some, like the Twenty-seventh, the Forty-second, the Forty-sixth, the Fifty-first, the Sixty-third, the Ninety-first, the Ninety-sixth, the One Hundred and Third, the One Hundred and Seventh, the One Hundred and Thirty-ninth, which rank with the noblest poetic literature of the world. Others move on a lower level, and show the traces of effort and constraint. There are also manifest alterations and interpolations, which are not always improvements. Dr. Perowne, who is one of the wisest and most conservative of modern commentators, says, "Many of the Psalms have not come down to us in their original form," * and refers to the alterations which the Seventieth makes in the Fortieth, and the Fifty-third in the Fourteenth. The last two verses of the Fifty-first were evidently added by a later hand. The whole book, in its pres-

* *The Book of Psalms.* 2 volumes, London, 1883. Volume I, page 82.

ent form, shows the marks of its compilation and use as the Hymn-Book of the Jewish people. Not only in the titles, but also in the text, we can discern the work of the compiler, critic, and adapter, sometimes wise, but occasionally otherwise.

IV

The most essential thing in the appreciation of the poetry in the Psalms is the recognition of the three great spiritual qualities which distinguish them.

The first of these is the deep and genuine love of nature. The psalmists delight in the vision of the world, and their joy quickens their senses to read both the larger hieroglyphs of glory written in the stars and the delicate tracings of transient beauty on leaf and flower; to hear both the mighty roaring of the sea and the soft sweet laughter of the rustling corn-fields. But in all these they see the handwriting and hear the voice of God. It is His presence that makes the world sublime and beautiful. The direct, piercing, elevating sense of this presence simplifies, enlarges, and ennobles their style, and makes it different from other nature-poetry. They never lose themselves, as Theocritus and Wordsworth and Shelley and Tennyson sometimes do, in the contemplation and description of natural beauty. They see it, but they always see beyond it. Compare, for example, a modern versified translation with the psalm itself:

> The spacious firmament on high,
> With all the blue ethereal sky
> And spangled heavens, a shining frame,
> Their Great Original proclaim.*

Addison's descriptive epithets betray a conscious effort to make a splendid picture. But the psalmist felt no need of this; a larger impulse lifted him at once into "the grand style:"

> The heavens declare the glory of God;
> And the firmament showeth his handiwork.

The second quality of the poetry in the Psalms is their passionate sense of the beauty of holiness. Keats was undoubtedly right in his suggestion that the poet must always see truth in the form of beauty. Otherwise he may be a philosopher, or a critic, or a

* Joseph Addison, 1712.

moralist, but he is not a true poet. But we must go on from this standpoint to the Platonic doctrine that the highest form of beauty is spiritual and ethical. The poet must also see beauty in the light of truth. It is the harmony of the soul with the eternal music of the Good. And the highest poets are those who, like the psalmists, are most ardently enamoured of righteousness. This fills their songs with sweetness and fire incomparable and immortal:

The fear of the Lord is clean, enduring for ever:
The judgments of the Lord are true and righteous alto-
gether.
More to be desired are they than gold, yea, than much
fine gold:
Sweeter also than honey and the honeycomb.

The third quality of the poetry of the Psalms is their intense joy in God. No lover ever poured out the longings of his heart toward his mistress more eagerly than the Psalmist voices his desire and thirst for God. No conqueror ever sang of victory more exultantly than the Psalmist rejoices in the Lord, who is his light and his salvation, the strength of his life and his portion forever.

After all, the true mission of poetry is to increase

joy. It must, indeed, be sensitive to sorrow and acquainted with grief. But it has wings given to it in order that it may bear us up into the air of gladness.

There is no perfect joy without love. Therefore love-poetry is the best. But the highest of all love-poetry is that which celebrates, with the Psalms,

> that Love which is and was
> My Father and my Brother and my God.

THE GOOD ENCHANTMENT OF
CHARLES DICKENS

THE GOOD ENCHANTMENT OF
CHARLES DICKENS

I

THERE are four kinds of novels.

First, those that are easy to read and hard to remember: the well-told tales of no consequence, the cream-puffs of perishable fiction.

Second, those that are hard to read and hard to remember: the purpose-novels which are tedious sermons in disguise, and the love-tales in which there is no one with whom it is possible to fall in love.

Third, those that are hard to read and easy to remember: the books with a crust of perverse style or faulty construction through which the reader must break in order to get at the rich and vital meaning.

Fourth, those that are easy to read and easy to remember: the novels in which stories worth telling are well-told, and characters worth observing are vividly painted, and life is interpreted to the imagination in enduring forms of literary art. These are the best-sellers which do not go out of print—everybody's books.

In this fourth class healthy-minded people and unprejudiced critics put the novels of Charles Dickens. For millions of readers they have fulfilled what Dr. Johnson called the purpose of good books, to teach us to enjoy life or help us to endure it. They have awakened laughter and tears. They have enlarged and enriched existence by revealing the hidden veins of humour and pathos beneath the surface of the every-day world, and by giving "the freedom of the city" to those poor prisoners who had thought of it only as the dwelling-place of so many hundred thousand inhabitants and no real persons.

What a city it was that Dickens opened to us! London, of course, in outward form and semblance, —the London of the early Victorian epoch, with its reeking Seven Dials close to its perfumed Piccadilly, with its grimy river-front and its musty Inns of Court and its mildly rural suburbs, with its rollicking taverns and its deadly solemn residential squares and its gloomy debtors' prisons and its gaily insanitary markets, with all its consecrated conventions and unsuspected hilarities,—vast, portentous, formal, merry, childish, inexplicable, a wilderness of human homes and haunts, ever thrilling with sincerest passion, mirth, and pain,—London it was, as the eye saw it in those days, and as the curious traveller may still retrace some of its vanishing landmarks and fading features.

But it was more than London, after Dickens touched it. It was an enchanted city, where the streets seemed to murmur of joy or fear, where the dark faces of the dens of crime scowled or leered at you, and the decrepit houses doddered in senility, and the new mansions stared you down with stolid pride. Everything spoke or made a sign to you. From red-curtained windows jollity beckoned. From prison-doors lean hands stretched toward you. Under bridges and among slimy piers the river gurgled, and chuckled, and muttered unholy secrets. Across trim front-yards little cottages smiled and almost nodded their good-will. There were no dead spots, no deaf and dumb regions. All was alive and significant. Even the real estate became personal. One felt that it needed but a word, a wave of the wand, to bring the buildings leaping, roistering, creeping, tottering, stalking from their places.

It was an enchanted city, and the folk who filled it and almost, but never quite, crowded it to suffocation, were so intensely and supernaturally human, so blackly bad, so brightly good, so touchingly pathetic, so supremely funny, that they also were creatures of enchantment and seemed to come from fairy-land.

For what is fairy-land, after all? It is not an invisible region, an impossible place. It is only the realm of the hitherto unobserved, the not yet realized, where the things we have seen but never noticed, and the persons we have met but never known, are suddenly "translated," like Bottom the Weaver, and sent forth upon strange adventures.

That is what happens to the Dickens people. Good or bad they surpass themselves when they get into his books. That rotund Brownie, Mr. Pickwick, with his amazing troupe; that gentle compound of Hop-o'-my-Thumb and a Babe in the

Wood, Oliver Twist, surrounded by wicked uncles, and hungry ogres, and good fairies in bottle-green coats; that tender and lovely Red Riding-Hood, Little Nell; that impetuous Hans-in-Luck, Nicholas Nickleby; that intimate Cinderella, Little Dorrit; that simple-minded Aladdin, Pip; all these, and a thousand more like them, go rambling through Dickensopolis and behaving naturally in a most extraordinary manner.

Things that have seldom or never happened, occur inevitably. The preposterous becomes the necessary, the wildly improbable is the one thing that must come to pass. Mr. Dombey is converted, Mr. Krook is removed by spontaneous combustion, Mr. Micawber performs amazing feats as an amateur detective, Sam Weller gets married, the immortally absurd epitaphs of Young John Chivery and Mrs. Sapsea are engraved upon monuments more lasting than brass.

The fact is, Dickens himself was bewitched by the spell of his own imagination. His people carried him away, did what they liked with him. He wrote of Little Nell: "You can't imagine how ex-

hausted I am to-day with yesterday's labours. I
went to bed last night utterly dispirited and done
up. All night I have been pursued by the child;
and this morning I am unrefreshed and miserable.
I don't know what to do with myself. . . . I think
the close of the story will be great." Again he says:
"As to the way in which these characters have
opened out [in *Martin Chuzzlewit*], that is to me
one of the most surprising processes of the mind in
this sort of invention. Given what one knows,
what one does not know springs up; and I am *as
absolutely certain of its being true, as I am of the
law of gravitation*—if such a thing is possible, more
so."

Precisely such a thing (as Dickens very well understood) is not only possible, but unavoidable.
For what certainty have we of the law of gravitation? Only by hearsay, by the submissive reception
of a process of reasoning conducted for us by Sir
Isaac Newton and other vaguely conceived men of
science. The fall of an apple is an intense reality
(especially if it falls upon your head); but the law
which regulates its speed is for you an intellectual

abstraction as remote as the idea of a "combination in restraint of trade," or the definition of "art for art's sake." Whereas the irrepressible vivacity of Sam Weller, and the unctuous hypocrisy of Pecksniff, and the moist humility of Uriah Heep, and the sublime conviviality of Dick Swiveller, and the triumphant make-believe of the Marchioness are facts of experience. They have touched you, and you cannot doubt them. The question whether they are actual or imaginary is purely academic.

Another fairy-land feature of Dickens's world is the way in which minor personages of the drama suddenly take the centre of the stage and hold the attention of the audience. It is always so in fairy-land.

In *The Tempest*, what are Prospero and Miranda, compared with Caliban and Ariel? In *A Midsummer Night's Dream*, who thinks as much of Oberon and Titania, as of Puck, and Bottom the Weaver? Even in an historical drama like Henry IV, we feel that Falstaff is the most historic character.

Dickens's first lady and first gentleman are often less memorable than his active supernumeraries.

A hobgoblin like Quilp, a good old nurse like Peggotty, a bad old nurse like Sairey Gamp, a volatile elf like Miss Mowcher, a shrewd elf and a blunder-headed elf like Susan Nipper and Mr. Toots, a good-natured disreputable sprite like Charley Bates, a malicious gnome like Noah Claypole, a wicked ogre like Wackford Squeers, a pair of fairy-godmothers like the Cheeryble Brothers, a dandy ouphe like Mr. Mantalini, and a mischievous, wooden-legged kobold like Silas Wegg, take stronger hold upon us than the Harry Maylies and Rose Flemings, the John Harmons and Bella Wilfers, for whose ultimate matrimonial felicity the business of the plot is conducted. Even the more notable heroes often pale a little by comparison with their attendants. Who remembers Martin Chuzzlewit as clearly as his servant Mark Tapley? Is Pip, with his Great Expectations, half as delightful as his clumsy dry-nurse Joe Gargery? Has even the great Pickwick a charm to compare with the unique, immortal Sam Weller?

Do not imagine that Dickens was unconscious of this disarrangement of rôles, or that it was an evi-

dence of failure on his part. He knew perfectly
well what he was doing. Great authors always do.
They cannot help it, and they do not care. Homer
makes Agamemnon and Priam the kings of his tale,
and Paris the first walking gentleman and Helen
the leading lady. But Achilles and Ajax and Hec-
tor are the bully boys, and Ulysses is the wise jest-
er, and Thersites the tragic clown. As for Helen,—

> The face that launched a thousand ships,
> And burnt the topless towers of Ilium—

her reputed pulchritude means less to us than the
splendid womanhood of Andromache, or the wit
and worth of the adorable matron Penelope.

Now this unconventionality of art, which disre-
gards ranks and titles, even those of its own making, and finds the beautiful and the absurd, the
grotesque and the picturesque, the noble and the
base, not according to the programme but according to the fact, is precisely the essence of good
enchantment.

Good enchantment goes about discovering the ass
in the lion's skin and the wolf in sheep's clothing,
the princess in the goose-girl and the wise man under

the fool's cap, the pretender in the purple robe and the rightful heir in rags, the devil in the belfry and the Redeemer among the publicans and sinners. It is the spirit of revelation, the spirit of divine sympathy and laughter, the spirit of admiration, hope, and love—or better still, it is simply the spirit of life.

When I call this the essence of good enchantment I do not mean that it is unreal. I mean only that it is *unrealistic*, which is just the opposite of unreal. It is not in bondage to the beggarly elements of form and ceremony. It is not captive to names and appearances, though it revels in their delightful absurdity. It knows that an idol is nothing, and finds all the more laughter in its pompous pretence of being something. It can afford to be merry because it is in earnest; it is happy because it has not forgotten how to weep; it is content because it is still unsatisfied; it is humble in the sense of unfathomed faults and exalted in the consciousness of inexhaustible power; it calls nothing common or unclean; it values life for its mystery, its surprisingness, and its divine reversals of human prejudice,—just like

Beauty and the Beast and the story of the Ugly
Duckling.

This, I say, is the essence of good enchantment;
and it is also the essence of true religion. "For God
hath chosen the foolish things of the world to confound the wise, and the weak things of the world
to confound the mighty, and base things of the
world and things which are despised, yea, and
*things which are not, to bring to naught things which
are.*"

This is also the essence of real democracy, which
is not a theory of government but a state of mind.

No one has ever expressed it better than Charles
Dickens did in a speech which he made at Hart-
ford, Connecticut, seventy years ago. "I have
faith," said he, "and I wish to diffuse faith in the
existence—yes, of beautiful things, even in those
conditions of society which are so degenerate, so
degraded and forlorn, that at first sight it would
seem as though it could only be described by a
strange and terrible reversal of the words of Scripture—God said let there be light, and there was
none. I take it that we are born, and that we hold

75

our sympathies, hopes, and energies in trust for the Many and not the Few. That we cannot hold in too strong a light of disgust and contempt, before our own view and that of others, all meanness, falsehood, cruelty, and oppression of every grade and kind. Above all, that nothing is high because it is in a high place; and that nothing is low because it is in a low place. This is the lesson taught us in the great book of Nature. This is the lesson which may be read alike in the bright track of the stars, and in the dusty course of the poorest thing that drags its tiny length upon the ground."

This was the creed of Dickens; and like every man's creed, conscious or unconscious, confessed or concealed, it made him what he was.

It has been said that he had no deep philosophy, no calmly reasoned and clearly stated theory of the universe. Perhaps that is true. Yet I believe he hardly missed it. He was too much interested in living to be anxious about a complete theory of life. Perhaps it would have helped him when trouble came, when domestic infelicity broke up his home, if he could have climbed into some philosopher's ivory tower. Perhaps not. I have observed that even the most learned and philosophic mortals, under these afflictions, sometimes fail to appreciate the consolations of philosophy to any noticeable extent. From their ivory towers they cry aloud, being in pain, even as other men.

But it was certainly not true (even though his biographer wrote it, and it has been quoted a thousand times), that just because Dickens cried aloud, "there was for him no 'city of the mind' against outward ills, for inner consolation and shelter." He was not cast out and left comfortless. Faith, hope, and charity—these three abode with him. His human sympathy, his indomitable imagination, his immense and varied interest in the strange adventures of men and women, his unfaltering intuition of the truer light of God that burns

> In this vexed beating stuffed and stopped-up brain,
> Heart, or whatever else——

these were the celestial powers and bright serviceable angels that built and guarded for him a true "city of refuge," secure, inviolate, ever open to the fugitive in the day of his calamity. Thither he could flee to find safety. There he could ungird his heart and indulge

Love and the thoughts that breathe for humankind;

there he could laugh and sing and weep with the children, the dream-children, which God had given him; there he could enter into his work-shop and shut the door and lose himself in joyous labour which should make the world richer by the gift of good books. And so he did, even until the end came and the pen fell from his fingers, he sitting safe in his city of refuge, learning and unfolding *The Mystery of Edwin Drood*.

O enchanted city, great asylum in the mind of man, where ideals are embodied, and visions take form and substance to parley with us! Imagination rears thy towers and Fancy populates thy streets; yet art thou a city that hath foundations, a dwelling eternal though unseen. Ever building, changing, never falling, thy walls are open-gated day and night. The fountain of youth is in thy gardens, the treasure of the humble in thy storehouses. Hope is thy doorkeeper, and Faith thy warden, and Love thy Lord. In thee the wanderer may take shelter and find himself by forgetting himself. In thee rest and refreshment are waiting for the weary, and new courage for the despondent, and new strength for the faint. From thy magic casements we have looked upon unknown horizons, and we return from thy gates to our task, our toil, our pilgrimage, with better and braver hearts, knowing more surely that the things which are seen were not made of things which do appear, and that the imperishable jewels of the universe are in the souls of men. O city of good enchantment, for my brethren and companions' sakes I will now say: Peace be within thee!

II

Of the outward appearance, or, as *Sartor Resartus* would have called it, the Time-Vesture and Flesh-Garment of that flaming light-particle which was cast hither from Heaven in the person of Charles Dickens, and of his ways and manners while he hasted jubilantly and stormfully across the astonished Earth, something must be said here.

Charles Dickens was born at Portsea, in 1812, an offspring of what the accurate English call the "lower middle class." Inheriting something from a father who was decidedly Micawberish, and a mother who resembled Mrs. Nickleby, Charles was not likely to be a humdrum child. But the remarkable thing about him was the intense, aspiring, and gaily sensible spirit with which he entered into the business of developing whatever gifts he had received from his vague and amiable parents.

The fat streak of comfort in his childish years, when his proud father used to stand the tiny lad on a table to sing comic songs for an applauding audience of relatives, could not spoil him. The lean streak of misery, when the improvident family sprawled in poverty, with its head in a debtors' prison, while the bright, delicate, hungry boy roamed the streets, or drudged in a dirty blacking-factory, could not starve him. The two dry years of school at Wellington House Academy could not fossilize him. The years from fifteen to nineteen, when he was earning his bread as office-boy, lawyers' clerk, shorthand reporter, could not commercialize him. Through it all he burned his way painfully and joyously.

He was not to be detailed as a perpetual comic songster in upholstered parlors; nor as a prosperous frock-coated citizen with fatty degeneration of the mind; nor as a newspaper politician, a power beneath the footstool. None of these alluring prospects delayed him. He passed them by, observing everything as he went, now hurrying, now sauntering, for all the world like a boy who has been sent somewhere. Where it was, he found out in his twenty-fifth year, when the extraordinary results of his self-education bloomed in the *Pickwick Papers* and *Oliver Twist*.

Never was a good thing coming out of Nazareth more promptly welcomed. The simple-minded critics of that day had not yet discovered the damning nature of popularity, and they hailed the new genius in spite of the fact that hundreds of thousands of people were reading his books. His success was exhilarating, overwhelming, and at times intoxicating.

It was roses, roses all the way.—

Some of them had thorns, which hurt his thin skin horribly, but they never made him despair or doubt the goodness of the universe. Being vexed, he let it off in anger instead of distilling it into pessimism to poison himself. Life was too everlastingly interesting for him to be long unhappy. A draught of his own triumph would restore him, a slice of his own work would reinvigorate him, and he would go on with his industrious dreaming.

No one enjoyed the reading of his books more than he the making of them, though he sometimes suffered keenly in the process. That was a proof of his faith that happiness does not consist in the absence of suffering, but in the presence of joy. Dulness, insincerity, stupid humbug—*voilà l'ennemi!* So he lived and wrote with a high hand and an outstretched arm. He made men see what he saw, and hate what he hated, and love what he loved. This was his great reward,—more than money, fame, or hosts of friends,—that he saw the children of his brain enter into the common life of the world.

But he was not exempt from the ordinary laws of nature. The conditions of his youth left their marks for good and evil on his maturity. The petting of his babyhood gave him the habit of showing

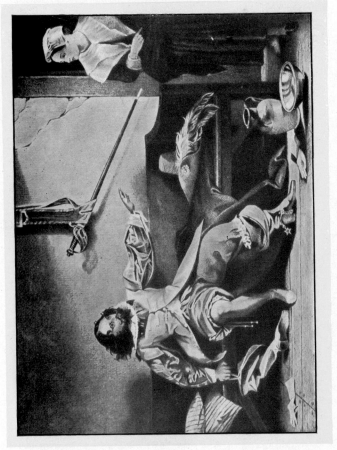

CHARLES DICKENS AS CAPTAIN BOBADIL IN "EVERY MAN IN HIS HUMOUR."
Painted by C. R. Leslie.

off. We often see him as a grown man, standing on the table and reciting his little piece, or singing his little song, to please an admiring audience. He delighted in playing to the galleries.

His early experience of poverty made him at once tremendously sympathetic and invincibly optimistic —both of which virtues belong to the poor more than to the rich. Dickens understood this and never forgot it. The chief moralities of his poor people are mutual helpfulness and unquenchable hopefulness. From them, also, he caught the tone of material comfort which characterizes his visions of the reward of virtue. Having known cold and hunger, he simply could not resist the desire to make his favourite characters—if they stayed on earth till the end of the book—warm and "comfy," and to give them plenty to eat and drink. This may not have been artistic, but it was intensely human.

The same personal quality may be noted in his ardour as a reformer. No writer of fiction has ever done more to better the world than Charles Dickens. But he did not do it by setting forth programmes of legislation and theories of government. As a matter of fact, he professed an amusing "contempt for the House of Commons," having been a Parliamentary reporter; and of Sir Robert Peel, who emancipated the Catholics, enfranchised the Jews, and repealed the Corn Laws, he thought so little that he caricatured him as Mr. Pecksniff.

Dickens felt the evils of the social order at the precise point where the shoe pinched; he did not go back to the place where the leather was tanned or the last designed. It was some practical abuse in poorhouses or police-courts or prisons; it was some hidden shame in the conduct of schools, or the renting of tenements; it was some monumental absurdity in the Circumlocution Office, some pompous and cruel delay in the course of justice, that made him hot with indignation. These were the things that he assailed with Rabelaisian laughter, or over which he wept with a deeper and more sincere pity than that of Tristram Shandy. His idea was that if he could get people to see that a thing was both ridiculous and cruel, they would want to stop it. What would come after that, he did not clearly know, nor had he any particularly valuable suggestions to make, except the general proposition that men should do justly, and love mercy, and walk humbly with their God.

He took no stock in the doleful predictions of the politicians that England was in an awful state merely because Lord Coodle was going out of office, and Sir Thomas Doodle would not come in, and each of these was the only man to save the country. The trouble seemed to him deeper and more real. It was a certain fat-witted selfishness, a certain callous, complacent blindness in the people who were likely to read his books. He conceived that his duty as a novelist was done when he had shown up the absurd and hateful things, and made people laugh at their ugliness, weep over their inhumanity, and long to sweep them away.

In this attitude, I think, Dickens was not only natural, and true to his bringing-up, but also wise as a great artist in literature. For I have observed that brilliant writers, while often profitable as satirists to expose abuses, are seldom judicious as legislators to plan reforms.

Before we leave this subject of the effects of

Dickens's early poverty and sudden popularity, we must consider his alleged lack of refinement. Some say that he was vulgar, others that he was ungrateful and inconsiderate of the feelings of his friends and relations, others that he had little or no taste. I should rather say, in the words of the old epigram, that he had a great deal of taste, and that some of it was very bad.

Take the matter of his caricaturing real people in his books. No one could object to his use of the grotesque insolence of a well-known London magistrate as the foundation of his portrait of Mr. Fang in *Oliver Twist*. That was public property. But the amiable eccentricities of his own father and mother, the airy irresponsible ways of his good friend Leigh Hunt, were private property. Yet even here Dickens could not reasonably be blamed for observing them, for being amused by them, or for letting them enrich his general sense of the immense, incalculable, and fantastic humour of the world. Taste, which is simply another name for the gusto of life, has a comic side; and a man who is keenly sensitive to everything cannot be expected

86

to be blind to the funny things that happen among his family and friends. But when Dickens used these private delights for the public amusement, and in such a form that the partial portraits of Mr. and Mrs. Micawber, Mrs. Nickleby, and Harold Skimpole were easily identified, all that we can say is that his taste was still there, but it had gone bad. What could you expect? Where, in his early years, was he likely to have learned the old-fashioned habit of reserve in regard to private affairs, which you may call either a mark of good manners, or a sign of silly pride, according to your own education?

Or take his behavior during his first visit to America in 1842, and immediately after his return to England. His reception was enough to turn anybody's head. "There never was a king or emperor," wrote Dickens to a friend, "so cheered and followed by crowds, and entertained at splendid balls and dinners, and waited upon by public bodies of all kinds." This was at the beginning. At the end he was criticized by all, condemned by many, and abused by some of the newspapers. Why? Chiefly because he used the dinners given in his honour as occasions to convict the Americans of their gross national sin of literary piracy, and because when he got home he wrote a book of *American Notes*, containing some very severe strictures upon the country which had just entertained him so magnificently.

Mr. Chesterton defends Dickens for his attack upon the American practice of book-stealing which grew out of the absence of an International Copyright Law. He says that it was only the new, raw sensibility of the Americans that was hurt by these speeches. "Dickens was not in the least desirous of being thought too 'high-souled' to want his wages. . . . He asked for his money in a valiant and ringing voice, like a man asking for his honour." And this, Mr. Chesterton leaves us to infer, is what any bold Englishman, as distinguished from a timidly refined American, would do.

Precisely. But if the bold Englishman had been gently-bred would he have accepted an invitation to dinner in order that he might publicly say to his host, in a valiant and ringing voice, "You owe me

a thousand pounds"? Such procedure at the din-
ner-table is contrary not only to good manners but
also to good digestion. This is what Mr. Chesterton's bold British constitution apparently prevents
him from seeing. What Dickens said about international copyright was right. But he was
wretchedly wrong in his choice of the time and
place for saying it. The natural irritation which
his bad taste produced was one of the causes which
delayed for fifty years the success of the efforts of
American authors to secure copyright for foreign
authors.

The same criticism applies to the *American Notes*.
Read them again and you will see that they are not
bad notes. With much that he says about Yankee
boastfulness and superficiality, and the evils of
slavery, and the dangers of yellow journalism, every
sane American will agree to-day. But the occasion
which Dickens took for making these remarks was
not happily chosen. It was as if a man who had
just been entertained at your house should write
to thank you for the pleasure of the visit, and im-
prove the opportunity to point out the shocking

defects of your domestic service and the exceedingly bad tone which pervaded your establishment. Such a "bread-and-butter letter" might be full of good morals, but their effect would be diminished by its bad manners. Of this Dickens was probably quite unconscious. He acted spontaneously, irrepressibly, vivaciously, in accordance with his own taste; and it surprised and irritated him immensely that people were offended by it.

It was precisely so in regard to his personal appearance. When the time suddenly arrived that he could indulge his taste in dress without fear of financial consequences, he did so hilariously and to the fullest extent. Here is a description of him as he appeared to an American girl at an evening party in Cincinnati eighty years ago. "He is young and handsome, has a mellow beautiful eye, fine brow and abundant hair. . . . His manner is easy and negligent, but not elegant. His dress was foppish. . . . He had a dark coat with lighter pantaloons; a black waistcoat embroidered with coloured flowers; and about his neck, covering his white shirt-front, was a black neck-cloth also embroidered with

colours, on which were two large diamond pins connected by a chain; a gold watch-chain and a large
red rose in his buttonhole completed his toilet."

The young lady does not seem to have been delighted with this costume. But Dickens did not
dress to please her, he dressed to please himself.
His taste was so exuberant that it naturally ef-
fervesced in this kind of raiment. There was certainly nothing immoral about it. He had paid for
it and he had a right to wear it, for to him it seemed
beautiful. He would have been amazed to know
that any young lady did not like it; and her opinion
would probably have had little effect upon him, for
he wrote of the occasion on which this candid girl
met him, as follows: "In the evening we went to
a party at Judge Walker's and were introduced to
at least one hundred and fifty first-rate bores, sepa-
rately and singly."

But what does it all amount to, this lack of dis-
cretion in manners, this want of reserve in speech,
this oriental luxuriance in attire? It simply goes
to show that *Dickens himself was a Dickens character*.

He was vivid, florid, inexhaustible, and untamed. There was material in the little man for a hundred of his own immortal caricatures. The self-portrait that he has drawn in *David Copperfield* is too smooth, like a retouched photograph. That is why David is less interesting than half-a-dozen other people in the book. If Dickens could have seen his own humourous aspects in the magic mirror of his fancy, it would have been among the richest of his observations, and if he could have let his enchantment loose upon the subject, not even the figures of Dick Swiveller and Harold Skimpole would have been more memorable than the burlesque of "Boz" by the hand of C. D.

But the humourous, the extravagant, the wildly picturesque,—would these have given a true and complete portrait of the man? Does it make any great difference what kind of clothes he wore, or how many blunders of taste and tact he made, even tragic blunders like his inability to refrain from telling the world all about his domestic unhappiness,—does all this count for much when we look back upon the wonders which his imagination wrought in fiction, and upon the generous fruits which his heart brought forth in life?

It is easy to endure small weaknesses when you can feel beneath them the presence of great and vital power. Faults are forgiven readily in one who has the genius of loving much. Better many blunders than the supreme mistake of a life that is

Faultily faultless, icily regular, splendidly null.

Charles Dickens never made, nor indeed was tempted to make, that mistake. He carried with him the defects of his qualities, the marks of his early life, the penalties of his bewildering success. But, look you, *he carried them*—they did not crush him nor turn him from his true course. Forward he marched, cheering and beguiling the way for his comrades with mirthful stories and tales of pity, lightening many a burden and consoling many a dark and lonely hour, until he came at last to the goal of honour and the haven of happy rest. Those who knew him best saw him most clearly as Carlyle did: "The good, the gentle, high-gifted, ever-friendly, noble Dickens,—every inch of him an Honest Man."

III

As an artist in fiction Dickens was great; but not because he had a correct theory of the technique of the novel, not because he always followed good rules and models in writing, nor because he was one

> Who saw life steadily and saw it whole.

On the contrary, his vision of life, though vivid, was almost always partial. He was capable of doing a great deal of bad work, which he himself liked. The plots of his novels, on which he toiled tremendously, are negligible; indeed it is often difficult to follow and impossible to remember them. The one of his books that is notably fine in structure and approximately faultless in technique—*A Tale of Two Cities*—is so unlike his other novels that it stands in a class by itself, as an example of what he could have done if he had chosen to follow that line. In a way it is his most perfect piece of work. But it is not his most characteristic piece of work, and therefore I think it has less value for us than some of his other books in which his peculiar, distinctive, unrivalled powers are more fully shown.

After all, art must not only interpret the world but also reveal the artist. The lasting interest of his vision, its distinction, its charm, depend, at least in some real degree, upon the personal touch. Being himself a part of the things that are seen, he must "paint the thing *as he sees it*" if he wishes to win the approval of "the God of things as they are."

Now the artistic value of Dickens's way of seeing things lay in its fitness to the purpose which he had in mind and heart,—a really great purpose, namely, to enhance the interest of life by good enchantment, to save people from the plague of dulness and the curse of indifference by showing them that the world is full of the stuff for hearty laughter and deep sympathy. This way of seeing things, with constant reference to their humourous and sentimental potency, was essential to the genius of Dickens. His method of making other people see it was strongly influenced, if not absolutely determined, by two facts which seemed to lie outside of his career as an author: first, his training as a reporter for the press; second, his favourite avocation as an amateur actor, stage-manager, and dramatic reader.

COMPANIONABLE BOOKS

The style of Dickens at its best is that of an inspired reporter. It is rapid, graphic, pictorial, aiming always at a certain heightening of effect, making the shadows darker and the lights brighter for the purpose of intensifying sensation. He did not get it in the study but in the street. Take his description in *Martin Chuzzlewit* of Todgers's Boarding House with its complicated smells and its mottled shades of dinginess; or take his picture in *Little Dorrit* of Marseilles burning in the August sunlight with its broad, white, universal stare. Here is the art of journalism,—the trick of intensification by omission,—carried to the limit. He aims distinctly at a certain effect, and he makes sure of getting it.

He takes long walks in the heart of London, attends police courts, goes behind the scenes of theatres, rides in omnibuses, visits prisons and workhouses. You think he is seeking realism. Quite wrong. He is seeking a sense of reality which shall make realism look cheap. He is not trying to put up canned goods which shall seem more or less like fresh vegetables. He is trying to extract the essential flavour of places and people so that you can taste it in a drop.

We find in his style an accumulation of details all bearing on a certain point; nothing that serves his purpose is overlooked; everything that is likely to distract the attention or obscure his aim is disregarded. The head-lines are in the text. When the brute, Bill Sykes, says to Nancy: "Get up," you know what is coming. When Mrs. Todgers gives a party to Mr. Pecksniff you know what is coming. But the point is that when it comes, tragedy or comedy, it is as pure and unadulterated as the most brilliant of reporters could make it.

Naturally, Dickens puts more emphasis upon the contrast between his characters than upon the contrast within them. The internal inconsistencies and struggles, the slow processes of growth and change which are the delight of the psychological novelist do not especially interest him. He sees things black or white, not gray. The objects that attract him most, and on which he lavishes his art, do not belong to the average, but to the extraordinary. Dickens is not a commonplace merchant.

He is a dealer in oddities and rarities, in fact the keeper of an "Old Curiosity Shop," and he knows how to set forth his goods with incomparable skill.

His drawing of character is sharp rather than deep. He makes the figure stand out, always recognizable, but not always thoroughly understood. Many of his people are simply admirable incarnations of their particular trades or professions: Mould the undertaker, old Weller the coachman, Tulkinghorn the lawyer, Elijah Program the political demagogue, Blimber the school-master, Stiggins the religious ranter, Betsey Prig the day-nurse, Cap'n Cuttle the retired skipper. They are all as easy to identify as the wooden image in front of a tobacconist's shop. Others are embodiments of a single passion or quality: Pecksniff of unctuous hypocrisy, Micawber of joyous improvidence, Mr. Toots of dumb sentimentalism, Little Dorrit of the motherly instinct in a girl, Joe Gargery of the motherly instinct in a man, Mark Tapley of resolute and strenuous optimism. If these persons do anything out of harmony with their head-lines, Dickens does not tell of it. He does not care for the incongruities, the modifications, the fine shadings which soften and complicate the philosophic and reflective view of life. He wants to write his "story" sharply, picturesquely, with "snap" and plenty of local colour; and he does it, in his happiest hours, with all the *verve* and skill of a star reporter for the *Morning Journal* of the Enchanted City.

In this graphic and emphatic quality the art of Dickens in fiction resembles the art of Hogarth in painting. But Dickens, like Hogarth, was much more than a reporter. He was a dramatist, and therefore he was also, by necessity, a moralist.

I do not mean that Dickens had a dramatic genius in the Greek sense that he habitually dealt with the eternal conflict between human passion and inscrutable destiny. I mean only this: that his lifelong love for the theatre often led him, consciously or unconsciously, to construct the *scenario* of a story with a view to dramatic effect, and to work up the details of a crisis precisely as if he saw it in his mind's eye on the stage.

Notice how the *dramatis personæ* are clearly marked as comic, or tragic, or sentimental. The moment they come upon the scene you can tell whether they are meant to appeal to your risibilities or to your sensibilities. You are in no danger of laughing at the heroine, or weeping over the funny man. Dickens knows too much to leave his audience in perplexity. He even gives to some of his personages set phrases, like the musical *motifs* of the various characters in the operas of Wagner, by which you may easily identify them. Mr. Micawber is forever "waiting for something to turn up." Mr. Toots always reminds us that "it's of no consequence." Sairey Gamp never appears without her imaginary friend Mrs. Harris. Mrs. General has "prunes and prism" perpetually on her lips.

Observe, also, how carefully the scene is set, and how wonderfully the preparation is made for a dramatic climax in the story. If it is a comic climax, like the trial of Mr. Pickwick for breach of promise, nothing is forgotten, from the hysterics of the obese Mrs. Bardell to the feigned indignation of Sergeant Buzfuz over the incriminating phrase "chops and tomato sauce!"

If it is a tragic climax, like the death of Bill Sykes,

a score of dark premonitions lead up to it, the dingiest slum of London is chosen for it, the grimy streets are filled with a furious crowd to witness it, and just as the murderer is about to escape, the ghostly eyes of his victim glare upon him, and he plunges from the roof, tangled in his rope, to be hanged by the hand of the Eternal Judge as surely as if he stood upon the gallows.

Or suppose the climax is not one of shame and terror, but of pure pity and tenderness, like the death of Little Nell. Then the quiet room is prepared for it, and the white bed is decked with winter berries and green leaves that the child loved because they loved the light; and gentle friends are there to read and talk to her, and she sleeps herself away in loving dreams, and the poor old grandfather, whom she has guided by the hand and comforted, kneels at her bedside, wondering why his dear Nell lies so still, and the very words which tell us of her peace and his grief, move rhythmically and plaintively, like soft music with a dying fall.

Close the book. The curtain descends. The drama is finished. The master has had his way with us; he has made us laugh; he has made us cry. We have been at the play.

But was it not as real to us while it lasted as many of the scenes in which we actors daily take our parts? And did it not mellow our spirits with mirth, and soften our hearts with tears? And now that it is over are we not likely to be a little better, a little kinder, a little happier for what we have laughed at or wept over?

Ah, master of the good enchantment, you have given us hours of ease and joy, and we thank you for them. But there is a greater gift than that. You have made us more willing to go cheerfully and companionably along the strange, crowded, winding way of human life, because you have deepened our faith that there is something of the divine on earth, and something of the human in heaven.

THACKERAY AND REAL MEN

THACKERAY AND REAL MEN

IN that fragrant bunch of *Theodore Roosevelt's Letters to His Children* which has just brightened and sweetened our too sadly strenuous times there are some passages on novel-reading which are full of spirited good sense. He says that he can read *Pendennis*, and *The Newcomes*, and *Vanity Fair* over and over again; he agrees with his boy in preferring Thackeray to Dickens, and then he gives the reason—or at least *a* reason—for this preference:

"Of course one fundamental difference . . . is that Thackeray was a gentleman and Dickens was not."

The damnatory clause in this sentence seems to me too absolute, though Roosevelt softens it by adding, "but a man might do some mighty good work without being in any sense a gentleman." That is certainly true, and beyond a doubt Dickens did it—a wonderful plenty of it. It is also true that in several perfectly good senses he was a brave and kind gentleman, despite his faults in manners and dress.

But it is the laudatory clause in Roosevelt's judgment that interests me. Thackeray's work is pervaded with his personality to an unusual degree. It is a saturated solution of the man. We can taste him in every page. And it is because we like the taste, because we find something strong and true, bracing and stimulant in it, that we love to read him. 'Tis like being with a gentleman in any enterprise or adventure; it gives us pleasure and does us unconscious good.

Well, then, what do we mean by "a gentleman?" Tennyson calls it

> The grand old name of gentleman
> Defamed by every charlatan,
> And soil'd with all ignoble use.

In the big New Oxford Dictionary there is more than a pageful of definitions of the word, and almost every English essayist has tried a shot at it. One thing is sure, its old hereditary use as a title of rank or property is going out, or already gone. "John Jones, Gent.," is a vanishing form of address. More and more the word is coming to connote something in character and conduct. Inheritance may enter into it, and the sense of honour has a great part in it, and its outward and visible sign is an unassuming fitness of behaviour in the various circumstances of life. But its indispensable essence is reality; its native speech, sincerity; and its controlling spirit, good-will.

Let us content ourselves with a description instead of a definition. A gentleman is a real man who deals honestly, bravely, frankly, and considerately with all sorts and conditions of other real men.

This is Thackeray's very mark and quality. We can feel it all through his life and works. Everything real in the world he recognized and accepted, even though he might not always like it. But the unreal people and things—the pretenders, the hypocrites, the shams, and the frauds (whether pious or impious)—he detested and scoffed away. Reality was his quest and his passion. He followed it with unfailing interest, penetration, and good temper. He found it, at least in humankind, always mixed and complicated, never altogether good nor altogether bad, no hero without a fault, and no villain without a germ of virtue. Life is really made that way. The true realist is not the materialist, the five-sense naturalist, but the man who takes into account the human soul and God as ultimate realities.

Thackeray's personal life had nothing that was remarkable and much that was admirable. It was simply the background of his genius. He was a child of the upper-middle class in England—if you know just what that means. He went to the Charterhouse School in London (which he afterward immortalized as Greyfriars in *The Newcomes*), and illustrated his passion for reality by getting his nose broken in a fight, which gave his face a permanent Socratic cast. At Cambridge University he seems to have written much and studied little, but that little to good purpose. He inherited a modest fortune, which he spent, not in riotous living, but in travel, art study in Paris, and in the most risky of all extravagances, the starting of new periodicals. When this failed and his money was gone, he lived in London as a hack-writer.

His young wife was taken from him by that saddest of all bereavements—the loss of her mind. It became necessary to place her in a private sanitarium, where she outlived her husband by thirty years. To her, and to the two little daughters whom she left him, Thackeray was faithful and devoted. He never complained, never flinched into an easy way of escape from his burden. He bent his back to it, and, in spite of natural indolence, he worked hard and was cheerful.

He made a host of friends and kept them, as Stevenson puts it, "without capitulation." Of course, this grim condition implies some frictions and some dislikes, and from these Thackeray was not exempt. The satire which was his first mode in writing was too direct and pungent to be relished by those who had any streak of self-humbug in their make-up. But, so far as I know, he had only one serious literary quarrel—that unhappy dispute with Mr. Edmund Yates, in which Dickens, with the best intentions in the world, became, unfortunately, somewhat involved. Thackeray might perhaps have been more generous and forgiving—he could have afforded that luxury. But he could not have been more honest and frank, more real, than he was. Being very angry, and for a just cause, he said so in plain words. Presently the tempest passed away. When Thackeray died in 1863, Dickens wrote:

"No one can be surer than I of the greatness and goodness of his heart."

The first period of his life as a man of letters was given almost entirely to satirical and fragmentary writing, under various *noms de guerre*. Hence, he remained for a long time in comparative poverty and obscurity, from which he stepped into fame and prosperity with the publication of his first large novel, *Vanity Fair*, in 1847–48. It was like turning the corner of Grub Street and coming into Glory Avenue.

Henceforth the way was open, though not easy. The succession of his big, welcome novels was slow, steady, unbroken. Each one brought him thousands of new readers, and the old ones were *semper fideles*, even when they professed a preference for the earlier over the later volumes. His lecture tours in Great Britain and the United States were eminently successful—more so, I think, than those of Charles Dickens. They may have brought in less money, but more of what old William Caxton, the prince of printers, called "good fame and renommee." The last of his completed books, and one of his most delightful, was *Roundabout Papers*— a volume of essays that has no superior in English for a light, firm, friendly touch upon the realities of life. His last story begun was *Denis Duval*, and on this he was working when he laid down his pen on Christmas Eve, 1863, and fell asleep for the last time.

It was Edmund Yates who wrote of him then:

"Thackeray was dead; and the purest English prose writer of the nineteenth century and the novelist with a greater knowledge of the human heart, as it really is, than any other—with the exception perhaps of Shakespeare and Balzac—was suddenly struck down in the midst of us."

The human heart as it really is—there's the point! That is what Thackeray sought to know, to understand, to reveal, and—no! not to explain, nor to judge and sentence—for that, as he well knew, was far beyond him or any of us—but his desire was to *show* the real heart of man, in its various complexities and perplexities, working its way through the divers realities and unrealities in which we are all entangled.

The acute French critic, Edmond Scherer, distinguished and divided between George Eliot as "a novelist of character," and Thackeray as "a novelist of manners." The epithet will pass only if we take the word in the sense of William of Wykeham's motto, "Manners makyth man."

For, as surely as there is something in the outward demeanour which unveils and discloses the person within, even so surely is there something in behaviour, the habitual mode of speech and conduct, which moulds the man using it. A false behaviour weaves a texture of lies into the warp of his nature. A true behaviour weakens the hold of his own self-delusions, and so helps him to know what he really is—which is good for him and for others.

It was in this sense that Thackeray was interested in manners, and depicted them in his books. Go with him to a ball, and you arrive at the hour of unmasking; to a club, and you are aware of the thoughts under the conversation; to a play, and you pass behind the footlights and the paint; to a death-bed, and—well, do you remember the death of Helen in *Pendennis?* and of the Colonel in *The Newcomes?* Foolish critics speak of these last two passages as "scenes." Scenes! By Heaven! no, they are realities. We can feel those pure souls passing.

Let us follow this clew of the passion for reality through the three phases of Thackeray's work.

I

At first he is the indefatigable satirist, rejoicing in the assault. Youth is almost always inclined that way—far more swift and sweeping in judgment, more severe in condemnation, than maturity or age. Thackeray writes much that is merely amusing, full of high spirits and pure fun, in his first period. But his main business is to expose false pretensions, false methods, false principles in literature and life; to show up the fakers, to ridicule the humbugs, to convict the crooks of every rank and degree.

113

Here, for example, is a popular fashion of books with criminals and burglars for heroes and heroines, portrayed in the glamour of romance. Very well, our satirist, assuming the name of "Ikey Solomons, Esq.," will take a real criminal, a murderess, and show us the manner of life she leads with her associates. So we have *Catherine*. Here is another fashion of weaving a fiction about a *chevalier d'industrie*, a bold, adventurous, conscienceless fellow who pursues his own pleasure with a swagger, and makes a brave show hide a mean and selfish heart. Very well, a fellow of this kidney shall tell his own story and show himself in his habit as he lives, and as he dies in prison. So we have *The Memoirs of Barry Lyndon, Esq.* Here are innumerable fashions of folly and falsehood current not only in high society, but also in the region of respectable mediocrity, and in the "world below-stairs." Very well, our satirist, under the name of "Jeames Yellowplush," or "M. Angelo Titmarsh," or "Fitz-Boodle," will show them up for us. So we have various bundles of short stories, and skits, and sketches of travel, some of them bubbling over with fun, some of them, like *Dennis Haggarty's Wife*, touched with quiet pathos.

The culmination of this satiric period is *The Book of Snobs*, which appeared serially in the London *Punch*, 1845–46. In order to understand the quality and meaning of Thackeray's satire—an element which stayed with him all through his writing, though it was later subdued to its proper place— we must take the necessary pains to know just what he meant by a "snob."

A snob is an unreal person who tries to pass himself off for a real person; a pretender who meanly admires and imitates mean things; an ape of gentility. He is a specific variety of the great genus "Sham." Carlyle, the other notable English satirist of the nineteenth century, attacked the whole genus with heavy artillery. Thackeray, with his light cavalry of ridicule, assailed the species.

All snobs are shams, but not all shams are snobs. The specific qualities of the snob are developed only in countries where there are social classes and distinctions, but no insuperable barriers between them. Thus in native India with its immutable caste, or

in Central Africa with its general barbarism, I fancy
it must be difficult to discover snobbism. (Yet I
have seen traces of it even among dogs and cats.)
But in a country like England or the United States
of America, where society is arranged in different
stories, with staircases between, snobbism is fre-
quent and flourishing.

*The snob is the man who tries to sneak up-stairs.
He is the surreptitious climber, the person who is
ashamed to pass for what he is.*

Has he been at an expensive college? He goes
home and snubs his old friends with allusions to
the distinguished society he has been keeping. Is
he entertaining fashionable strangers? He gives
them elaborate and costly fare at the most aurivo-
rous hotel, but at home his wife and daughters may
starve. He talks about books that he has never
read, and pretends to like music that sends him to
sleep. At his worst, he says his prayers on the
street-corners and reviles his neighbour for sins
which he himself cherishes in secret.

That is the snob: the particular species of sham
whom Thackeray pursues and satirizes through all

his disguises and metamorphoses. He does it un-
sparingly, yet never—or at least hardly ever—
savagely. There is always a strain of good humour
in it, and often a touch of fellow-feeling for the man
himself, camouflaged under his affectations. It may
not be worth while—this kind of work. All satire
is perishable. It has no more of the immortal in
it than the unreality which it aims to destroy. But
some shams die hard. And while they live and
propagate, the arrows which hit them fairly are not
out of date.

Stevenson makes a curious misjudgment of this
part of Thackeray's work, when he says in his essay
on "Some Gentlemen in Fiction":

"Personally [Thackeray] scarce appeals to us as
the ideal gentleman; if there were nothing else,
perpetual nosing after snobbery at least suggests
the snob."

Most true, beloved R. L. S., but did you forget
that this is precisely what Thackeray himself says?
He tells us not to be too quick or absolute in our
judgments; to acknowledge that we have some
faults and failings of our own; to remember that

other people have sometimes hinted at a vein, a trace, a vestige of snobbery in ourselves. Search for truth and speak it; but, above all, no arrogance —*faut pas monter sur ses grands chevaux*. Have you ever read the end of the lecture on "Charity and Humour"?

"The author . . . has been described by *The London Times* newspaper as a writer of considerable parts, but a dreary misanthrope, who sees no good anywhere, who sees the sky above him green, I think, instead of blue, and only miserable sinners around him. *So we are, as is every writer and reader I have heard of; so was every being who ever trod this earth, save One.* I cannot help telling the truth as I view it, and describing what I see. To describe it otherwise than it seems to me would be falsehood in that calling in which it has pleased Heaven to place me; treason to that conscience which says that men are weak; that truth must be told; that faults must be owned; that pardon must be prayed for; and that Love reigns supreme over all."

THACKERAY AND REAL MEN

II

With *Vanity Fair* begins what some one has called the *quadrilateral* on which Thackeray's larger fame rests. The three other pillars are, *Henry Esmond*, *Pendennis*, and *The Newcomes*. Which is the greatest of these four novels? On this question there is dispute among critics, and difference of opinion, even among avowed Thackerayans, who confess that they "like everything he wrote." Why try to settle the question? Why not let the interesting, illuminating *causerie* run on? In these furious days when the hysteria of world-problems vexes us, it is good to have some subjects on which we can dispute without ranting or raving.

For my part, I find *Vanity Fair* the strongest, *Pendennis* the most intimate, *The Newcomes* the richest and in parts the most lovable, and *Henry Esmond* the most admirable and satisfying, among Thackeray's novels. But they all have this in common: they represent a reaction from certain false fashions in fiction which prevailed at that time. From the spurious romanticism of G. P. R. James and Harrison Ainsworth, from the philosophic affectation of Bulwer, from the gilding and rococo-work of the super-snob Disraeli—all of them popular writers of their day—Thackeray turned away, not now as in his earlier period to satirize and ridicule and parody them, but to create something in a different *genre*, closer to the facts of life, more true to the reality of human nature.

We may read in the preface to *Pendennis* just what he had in mind and purpose:

"Many ladies have remonstrated and subscribers left me, because, in the course of the story, I described a young man resisting and affected by temptation. My object was to say, that he had the passions to feel, and the manliness and generosity to overcome them. You will not hear—it is best to know it—what moves in the real world, what passes in society, in the clubs, colleges, mess-rooms—what is the life and talk of your sons. A little more frankness than is customary has been attempted in this story; with no bad desire on the author's part, it is hoped, and with no ill consequence to any reader. If truth is not always pleasant, at any rate truth is

Reproduced from the Kensington Edition of Thackeray's Works.

WILLIAM MAKEPEACE THACKERAY.

best, from whatever chair—from those whence graver writers or thinkers argue, as from that at which the story-teller sits as he concludes his labour, and bids his kind reader farewell."

It is amusing, in this age of art undressed, to read this modest defense of frankness in fiction. Its meaning is very different from the interpretation of it which is given by disciples of the "show-every-thing-without-a-fig-leaf" school.

Thackeray did not confuse reality with indecency. He did not think it needful to make his hero cut his toe-nails or take a bath in public in order to show him as a real man. The ordinary and common physical details of life may be taken for granted; to obtrude them is to exaggerate their importance. It is with the frailties and passions, the faults and virtues, the defeats and victories of his men and women that Thackeray deals. He describes Pendennis tempted without making the description a new temptation. He brings us acquainted with Becky Sharp, *enchanteresse*, without adding to her enchantment. We feel that she is capable of anything; but we do not know all that she actually

121

did,—indeed Thackeray himself frankly confessed that even he did not know, nor much care.

The excellence of his character-drawing is that his men and women are not mere pegs to hang a doctrine or a theory on. They have a life of their own, independent of, and yet closely touching his. This is what he says of them in his essay "*De Finibus*":

"They have been boarding and lodging with me for twenty months. . . . I know the people utterly,—I know the sound of their voices."

Fault has been found with him (and that by such high authority as Mr. Howells) for coming into his own pages so often with personal comment or, "a word to the reader." It is said that this disturbs the narrative, breaks the illusion, makes the novel less convincing as a work of art. Frankly, it does not strike me that way. On the contrary, it adds to the verisimilitude. These men and women are so real to him that he cannot help talking to us about them as we go along together. Is it not just so in actual life, when you go with a friend to watch the passing show? Do you think that what Thackeray says to you about Colonel Newcome, or Captain Costigan, or Helen Pendennis, or Laura, or Ethel, or George Warrington, makes them fade away?

Yes, I know the paragraphs at the beginning and end of *Vanity Fair* about the showman and the puppets and the box. But don't you see what the parable means? It is only what Shakespeare said long ago:

> All the world's a stage,
> And all the men and women merely players.

Nor would Thackeray have let this metaphor pass without adding to it Pope's fine line:

> Act well your part, there all the honour lies.

Of course, there is another type of fiction in which running personal comment by the author would be out of place. It is illustrated in Dickens by *A Tale of Two Cities*, and in Thackeray by *Henry Esmond*. The latter seems to me the most perfect example of a historical novel in all literature. More than that,—it is, so far as I know, the best portrayal of the character of a gentleman.

123

The book presents itself as a memoir of Henry Esmond, Esq., a colonel in the service of her Majesty, Queen Anne, written by himself. Here, then, we have an autobiographical novel, the most difficult and perilous of all modes of fiction. If the supposed author puts himself in the foreground, he becomes egotistical and insufferable; if he puts himself in the background, he becomes insignificant, a mere Chinese "property-man" in the drama. This dilemma Thackeray avoids by letting Esmond tell his own story in the third person—that is to say, with a certain detachment of view, such as a sensible person would feel in looking back on his own life.

Rarely is this historic method of narration broken. I recall one instance, in the last chapter, where Beatrix, after that tremendous scene in the house of Castlewood with the Prince, reveals her true nature and quits the room in a rage. The supposed author writes:

"Her keen words gave no wound to Mr. Esmond; his heart was too hard. As he looked at her, he wondered that he could ever have loved her. . . .

The Prince blushed and bowed low, as she gazed at him and quitted the chamber. *I have never seen her from that day.*"

Thackeray made this slip on purpose. He wanted us to feel the reality of the man who is trying to tell his own story in the third person.

This, after all, is the real value of the book. It is not only a wonderful picture of the Age of Queen Anne, its ways and customs, its manner of speech and life, its principal personages—the red-faced queen, and peremptory Marlborough, and smooth Atterbury, and rakish Mohun, and urbane Addison, and soldier-scholar Richard Steele—appearing in the background of the political plot. It is also, and far more significantly, a story of the honour of a gentleman—namely, Henry Esmond—carried through a life of difficulty, and crowned with the love of a true woman, after a false one had failed him.

Some readers profess themselves disappointed with the dénouement of the love-story. They find it unnatural and disconcerting that the hero should win the mother and not the daughter as the guerdon of his devotion. Not I. Read the story more closely.

When it opens, in the house of Castlewood, Esmond is a grave, lonely boy of twelve; Lady Castlewood, fair and golden-haired, is in the first bloom of gracious beauty, twenty years old; Beatrix is a dark little minx of four years. Naturally, Henry falls in love with the mother rather than with the daughter, grows up as her champion and knight, defends her against the rakishness of Lord Mohun, resolves for her sake to give up his claim to the title and the estate. Then comes the episode of his infatuation by the wonderful physical beauty of Beatrix, the vixen. That madness ends with the self-betrayal of her letter of assignation with the Prince, and her subsequent conduct. Esmond returns to his first love, his young love, his true love, Lady Castlewood. Of its fruition let us read his own estimate:

"That happiness which hath subsequently crowned it, cannot be written in words; it is of its nature sacred and secret, and not to be spoken of, though the heart be ever so full of thankfulness, save to Heaven and the One Ear alone—to one fond being, the truest and tenderest and purest wife ever man was blessed with."

III

I have left myself scant space to speak of Thackeray's third phase in writing—his work as a moralist. But perhaps this is well, for, as he himself said, (and as I have always tried to practise), the preacher must be brief if he wishes to be heard. Five words that go home are worth more than a thousand that wander about the subject.

Thackeray's direct moralizings are to be found chiefly in his lectures on "The Four Georges," "The English Humourists," and in the "Roundabout Papers." He was like Lowell: as a scholastic critic he was far from infallible, but as a vital interpreter he seldom missed the mark.

After all, the essential thing in life for us as real men is to have a knowledge of facts to correct our follies, an ideal to guide our efforts, and a gospel to sustain our hopes.

That was Thackeray's message as moralist. It

is expressed in the last paragraph of his essay "*Nil Nisi Bonum*," written just after the death of Macaulay and Washington Irving:

"If any young man of letters reads this little sermon—and to him, indeed, it is addressed—I would say to him, 'Bear Scott's words in your mind, and *be good, my dear.*' Here are two literary men gone to their account, and, *laus Deo*, as far as we know, it is fair, and open, and clean. Here is no need of apologies for shortcomings, or explanations of vices which would have been virtues but for unavoidable, etc. Here are two examples of men most differently gifted—each pursuing his calling; each speaking his truth as God bade him; each honest in his life; just and irreproachable in his dealings; dear to his friends; honoured by his country; beloved at his fireside. It has been the fortunate lot of both to give incalculable happiness and delight to the world, which thanks them in return with an immense kindliness, respect, affection. It may not be our chance, brother scribe, to be endowed with such merit, or rewarded with such fame. But the rewards of these men are rewards paid to *our service*.

We may not win the bâton or epaulettes; but **God** give us strength to guard the honour of the flag!"

With this supplication for myself and for others, I leave this essay on Thackeray, the greatest of English novelists, to the consideration of real men.

GEORGE ELIOT AND REAL WOMEN

GEORGE ELIOT AND REAL
WOMEN

GEORGE ELIOT was a woman who wrote full-grown novels for men.

Other women have done and are doing notable work in prose fiction—Jane Austen, George Sand, Charlotte Brontë, Mrs. Stowe, Margaret Deland, Edith Wharton, Katharine Fullerton Gerould, Mrs. Humphry Ward—the list might easily be extended, but it would delay us from the purpose of this chapter. Let me rather make a general salute to all the sisterhood who have risen above the indignity of being called "authoresses," and, without pursuing perilous comparisons, go directly to the subject in hand.

What was it that enabled George Eliot to enter the field of the English novel at a time when Dickens and Thackeray were at the height of their fame, and win a place in the same class with them?

It was certainly not the hide-and-seek of the sex

of the new writer under a pseudonym. You remember, opinions were divided on this question. Carlyle and Thackeray thought that the author of *Scenes of Clerical Life* was a man. Dickens was sure that it was a woman. But a mystification of this kind has no interest apart from the primary value of the works of the unidentified writer in question. Nor does it last long as an advertisement, unless the following books excel the first; and, in that case, the secret is sure to be soon discovered.

George Eliot's success and distinction as a novelist were due to three things: first, the preliminary and rather obvious advantage of having genius; second, a method of thinking and writing which is commonly (though perhaps arrogantly) called masculine; third, a quickness of insight into certain things, a warmth of sympathy for suffering, and an instinct of sacrifice which we still regard (we hope rightly) as feminine. A man for logic, a woman for feeling, a genius for creative power—that was a great alliance. But the womanhood kept the priority without which it would not only have died out, but also have endangered, in dying, the other qualities. Dickens was right when he said of certain touches in the work of this pseudonymous writer: "If they originated with no woman, I believe that no man ever before had the art of making himself mentally so like a woman since the world began."

George Eliot's profile resembled Savonarola's. He was one of her heroes. But she was not his brother. She was his sister in the spirit.

Her essential femininity was the reason why the drawing of her women surpassed the drawing of her men. It was more intimate, more revealing, more convincing. She knew women better. She painted them of many types and classes—from the peasant maid to the well-born lady, from the selfish white cat to the generous white swan-sister; from the narrow-minded Rosamund to the deep-hearted, broad-minded Romola; all types, I think, but one—the lewdly carnal Circe. In all her books, with perhaps a single exception, it is a woman who stands out most clearly from the carefully studied and often complex background as the figure of interest. And even in that one it is the slight form of Eppie, the golden-hearted girl who was sent to save old Silas Marner from melancholy madness, that shines brightest in the picture.

The finest of her women—finest not in the sense of being faultless, but of having in them most of that wonderful sacrificial quality which Goethe called *das ewig Weibliche*—were those upon whose spiritual portraits George Eliot spent her most loving care and her most graphic skill.

She shows them almost always in the revealing light of love. But she does not dwell meticulously on the symptoms or the course of the merely physical attraction. She knows that it is there; she confesses that it is potent. But it seems to her, (as indeed it really is,) far more uniform and less interesting than the meaning of love in the *soul* of a woman as daughter, sister, sweetheart, wife. Were it not for that inward significance there would be little to differentiate the physical act from the mating of the lower animals—an affair so common and casual that it merits less attention than some writers give it. But in the inner life of thought and emotion, in a woman's intellectual and moral nature,—

there love has its mystery and its power, there it
brings deepest joy or sharpest sorrow, there it
strengthens or maims.

It is because George Eliot knows this and reveals
it with extraordinary clearness that her books have
an especial value. Other qualities they have, of
course, and very high qualities. But this is their
proper and peculiar excellence, and the source, if I
mistake not, of their strongest appeal to sanely
thinking men.

The Man Who Understood Woman is the title of
a recent clever trivial story. But of course such a
man is a myth, an impostor, or a self-deluder. He
makes a preposterous claim.

Thackeray and Dickens, for example, made no
such pretension. Some of their women are admirably drawn; they are very lovable, or very despicable, as the case may be; but they are not completely
convincing. Thackeray comes nearer than Dickens,
and George Meredith, I think, much nearer than
either of the others. But in George Eliot we feel
that we are listening to one who does understand.
Her women, in their different types, reveal some-

thing of that thinking, willing, feeling other-half of humanity with whom man makes the journey of life. They do not cover all the possibilities of variation in the feminine, for these are infinite, but they are real women, and so they have an interest for real men.

Let us take it for granted that we know enough of the details of George Eliot's life to enable us to understand and appreciate certain things in her novels. Such biographical knowledge is illuminating in the study of the works of any writer. The author of a book is not an algebraic quantity nor a strange monster, but a human being with certain features and a certain life-history.

But, after all, the promotion of literary analysis is not the object of these chapters. Plain reading, and the pleasure of it, is what I have in mind. For that cause I love most of George Eliot's novels, and am ready to maintain that they are worthy to be loved. And so, even if my "taken for granted" a few lines above should not be altogether accurate in these days of ignorant contempt of all that is

"Victorian," I may still go ahead to speak of her books as they are in themselves: strong, fine, rewarding pieces of English fiction: that is what they would remain, no matter who had written them.

It must be admitted at once that they are not adapted to readers who like to be spared the trouble of thinking while they read. They do not belong to the class of massage-fiction, Turkish-bath novels. They require a certain amount of intellectual exercise; and for this they return, it seems to me, an adequate recompense in the pleasurable sense of quickened mental activity and vigour.

But this admission must not be taken to imply that they are obscure, intricate, enigmatical, "tough reading," like the later books of George Meredith and Henry James, in which a minimum of meaning is hidden in a maximum of obfuscated verbiage, and the reader is invited to a tedious game of hunt-the-slipper. On the contrary, George Eliot at her best is a very clear writer—decidedly not shallow, nor superficial, nor hasty,—like the running comment which is supposed to illuminate the scenes in a moving-picture show,—but intentionally lucid and perspicuous. Having a story to tell, she takes pains to tell it so that you can follow it, not only in its outward, but also in its inward movement. Having certain characters to depict (and almost always mixed characters of good and evil mingled and conflicting as in real life), she is careful to draw them so that you shall feel their reality and take an interest in their strifes and adventures.

They are distinctly persons, capable of making their own choice between the worse and the better reason, and thereafter influenced by the consequences of that choice, which, if repeated, becomes a habit of moral victory or defeat. They are not puppets in the hands of an inscrutable Fate, like most of the figures in the books of the modern Russian novelists and their imitators. What do I care for the ever-so realistically painted marionettes in the fiction of Messrs. Gawky, Popoff, Dropoff, and Slumpoff? What interest have I in the minute articulations of the dingy automatons of Mijnheer Couperus, or the dismal, despicable figures who are pulled through the pages of Mr. Samuel Butler's *The Way of All Flesh*? A claim on compassion they might have if they were alive. But being, by the avowal of their creators, nothing more than imaginary bundles of sensation, helpless playthings of irresistible hereditary impulse and entangling destiny, their story and their fate leave me cold. What does it matter what becomes of them? They can neither be saved nor damned. They can only be drifted. There is no more human interest in them than there is in the predestined saints and foredoomed sinners of a certain type of Calvinistic theology.

But this is not George Eliot's view of life. It is not to her "a tale told by an idiot, full of sound and fury signifying nothing." Within the fixed circle of its stern natural and moral laws there is a hidden field of conflict where the soul is free to discern and choose its own cause, and to fight for it or betray it. However small that field may be, while it exists life has a meaning, and personalities are real, and the results of their striving or surrendering, though rarely seen complete or final, are worth following and thinking about. Thus George Eliot's people—at least the majority of them—have the human touch which justifies narrative and comment. We follow the fortunes of Dinah Morris and of Maggie Tulliver, of Romola, and of Dorothea Brooke—yes, and of Hetty Sorrel and Rosamund Vincy—precisely because we feel that they are real women and that the turning of their ways will reveal the secret of their hearts.

It is a mistake to think (as a recent admirable essay of Professor W. L. Cross seems to imply) that the books of George Eliot are characteristically novels of argument or propaganda. Once only, or perhaps twice, she yielded to that temptation and spoiled her story. But for the rest she kept clear of the snare of *Tendenz*.

Purpose-novels, like advertisements, belong in the temporary department. As certain goods and wares go out of date, and the often eloquent announcements that commended them suddenly disappear; even so the "burning questions" of the hour and age burn out, and the solutions of them presented in the form of fiction fall down with the other ashes. They have served their purpose, well or ill, and their transient importance is ended.

What endures, if anything, is the human story vividly told, the human characters graphically depicted. These have a permanent value. These belong to literature. Here I would place *Adam Bede* and *Silas Marner* and *The Mill on the Floss* and *Middlemarch*, because they deal with problems which never grow old; but not *Robert Elsmere*, because it deals chiefly with a defunct controversy in Biblical criticism.

George Eliot was thirty-eight years old when she made the amazing discovery that she was by nature, not what she had thought herself, a philosophical essayist and a translator of arid German treatises against revealed religion, but something very different—a novelist of human souls, and especially of the souls of women. It was the noteworthy success of her three long short stories, *Amos Barton*, *Mr. Gilfil's Love Story*, and *Janet's Repentance*, printed in *Blackwood's Magazine* in 1857, that revealed her to herself and to the world.

"Depend upon it, [she says to her imaginary reader in the first of these stories,] you would gain unspeakably if you would learn with me to see

143

something of the poetry and the pathos, the tragedy and the comedy, lying in the experience of the human soul that looks out through dull gray eyes and speaks in a voice of quite ordinary tones."

It was the interior drama of human life that attracted her interest and moved her heart with pity and fear, laughter and love. She found it for the most part in what we should call mediocre surroundings and on rather a humble and obscure stage. But what she found was not mediocre. It was the same discovery that Wordsworth made:

"A grandeur in the beatings of the heart."

By this I do not mean to say that a close study of the humanness of human nature, a searching contemplation of character, an acute and penetrating psychological analysis is all that there is in her novels. This is her predominant interest, beyond a doubt. She belongs to the school of Hawthorne, Henry James, Thomas Hardy—realists or romancers of the interior life. But she has other interests; and there are other things to reward us in the reading of her books.

There is, first of all, an admirable skill in the set-ting of her stories. No other novelist has described English midland landscape, towns, and hamlets, better than she. No other writer has given the rich, history-saturated scenery of Florence as well.

She is careful also not to exclude from her stage that messenger of relief and contrast whom George Meredith calls "the comic spirit." Shakespeare's clowns, wonderful as some of them are, seem at times like supernumeraries. They come in to make a "diversion." But George Eliot's rustic wits and conscious or unconscious humourists belong to the story. Mrs. Poyser and Bartle Massey, Mrs. Glegg and Mrs. Tulliver and Bob Jakin, could not be spared.

And then, her stories are really stories. They have action. They move; though sometimes, it must be confessed, they move slowly. Not only do the characters develop, one way or the other, but the plot also develops. Sometimes it is very simple, as in *Silas Marner;* sometimes it is extremely com-plicated, as in *Middlemarch*, where three love-stories are braided together. One thing it never is

145

—theatrical. Yet at times it moves into an intense scene, like the trial of Hetty Sorrel or the death of Tito Melema, in which the very essence of tragedy is concentrated.

From the success of *Scenes of Clerical Life* George Eliot went on steadily with her work in fiction, never turning aside, never pausing even, except when her health compelled, or when she needed time to fill her mind and heart with a new subject. She did not write rapidly, nor are her books easy to read in a hurry.

It was an extraordinary series: *Adam Bede* in 1859, *The Mill on the Floss* in 1860, *Silas Marner* in 1861, *Romola* in 1863, *Felix Holt, the Radical* in 1866, *Middlemarch* in 1871, *Daniel Deronda* in 1876; no padding, no "seconds," each book apparently more successful, certainly more famous, than its predecessor. How could one woman produce so much closely wrought, finely finished work? Of what sturdy mental race were the serious readers who welcomed it and found delight in it?

Mr. Oscar Browning of Cambridge said that *Daniel Deronda* was the climax, "the sun and glory of George Eliot's art." From that academic judgment I venture to dissent. It is a great book, no doubt, the work of a powerful intellect. But to me it was at the first reading, and is still, a tiresome book. Tediousness, which is a totally different thing from seriousness, is the unpardonable defect in a novel. It may be my own fault, but Deronda seems to me something of a prig. Now a man may be a prig without sin, but he ought not to take up too much room. Deronda takes up too much room. And Gwendolen Harleth, who dressed by preference in sea-green, seems to me to have a soul of the same colour—a psychological mermaid. She is unconvincing. I cannot love her. The vivid little Jewess, Mirah, is the only character with charm in the book.

Middlemarch is noteworthy for its extraordinary richness of human observation and the unexcelled truthfulness of some of its portraits. Mr. Isaac Casaubon is the living image of the gray-minded scholar and gentleman,—as delicately drawn as one of Miss Cecelia Beaux' portraits of aged, learned, wrinkled men. Rosamund Vincy is the typical "daughter of the horse-leech" in respectable clothes and surroundings. Dorothea Brooke is one of George Eliot's finest sacrificial heroines:

"A perfect woman, nobly plann'd."

The book, as a whole, seems to me to have the defect of superabundance. There is too much of it. It is like one of the late William Frith's large canvases, "The Derby Day," or "The Railway Station." It is constructed with skill, and full of rich material, but it does not compose. You cannot see the people for the crowd. Yet there is hardly a corner of the story in which you will not find something worth while.

Felix Holt, the Radical is marred, at least for me, by a fault of another kind. It is a novel of problem, of purpose. I do not care for problem-novels, unless the problem is alive, and even then I do not care very much for political economy in that form. It is too easy for the author to prove any proposition by attaching it to a noble character, or to disprove any theory by giving it an unworthy advocate. English radicalism of 1832 has quite passed away, or gone into the Coalition Cabinet. All that saves *Felix Holt* now (as it seems to me, who read novels primarily for pleasure) is the lovely figure of Esther Lyon, and her old father, a preacher who really was good.

Following the path still backward, we come to something altogether different. *Romola* is a historical romance on the grand scale. In the central background is the heroic figure of Savonarola, saintly but not impeccable; in the middle distance, a crowd of Renaissance people immersed in the rich and bloody turmoil of that age; in the foreground, the sharp contrast of two epic personalities—Tito Melema, the incarnation of smooth, easy-going selfishness which never refuses a pleasure nor accepts a duty; and Romola, the splendid embodiment of pure love in self-surrendering womanhood. The shameful end of Tito, swept away by the flooded river Arno and finally choked to death by the father whom he had disowned and wronged, has in it the sombre tone of Fate. But the end of the book is not defeat; it is triumph. Romola, victor through selfless courage and patience, saves and protects

149

the deserted mistress and children of her faithless husband. In the epilogue we see her like *Notre Dame de Secours*, throned in mercy and crowned with compassion.

Listen to her as she talks to Tito's son in the loggia looking over Florence to the heights beyond Fiesole.

" 'What is it, Lillo?' said Romola, pulling his hair back from his brow. Lillo was a handsome lad, but his features were turning out to be more massive and less regular than his father's. The blood of the Tuscan peasant was in his veins.

" 'Mamma Romola, what am I to be?' he said, well contented that there was a prospect of talking till it would be too late to con *Spirto gentil* any longer.

" 'What should you like to be, Lillo? You might be a scholar. My father was a scholar, you know, and taught me a great deal. That is the reason why I can teach you.'

" 'Yes,' said Lillo, rather hesitatingly. 'But he is old and blind in the picture. Did he get a great deal of glory?'

" 'Not much, Lillo. The world was not always very kind to him, and he saw meaner men than himself put into higher places, because they could flatter and say what was false. And then his dear son thought it right to leave him and become a monk; and after that, my father, being blind and lonely, felt unable to do the things that would have made his learning of greater use to men, so that he might still have lived in his works after he was in his grave.'

" 'I should not like that sort of life,' said Lillo. 'I should like to be something that would make me a great man, and very happy besides—something that would not hinder me from having a good deal of pleasure.'

" 'That is not easy, my Lillo. It is only a poor sort of happiness that could ever come by caring very much about our own narrow pleasures. We can only have the highest happiness, such as goes along with being a great man, by having wide thoughts, and feeling for the rest of the world as well as ourselves; and this sort of happiness often brings so much pain with it, that we can only tell it from pain by its being what we would choose before everything else, because our souls see it is good. There are so many things wrong and difficult in the world, that no man can be great—he can hardly keep himself from wickedness—unless he gives up thinking much about pleasure or rewards, and gets strength to endure what is hard and painful. My father had the greatness that belongs to integrity; he chose poverty and obscurity rather than falsehood. And there was Fra Girolamo—you know why I keep to-morrow sacred: *he* had the greatness which belongs to a life spent in struggling against powerful wrong, and in trying to raise men to the highest deeds they are capable of. And so, my Lillo, if you mean to act nobly and seek to know the best things God has put within reach of men, you must learn to fix your mind on that end, and not on what will happen to you because of it. And remember, if you were to choose something lower, and make it the rule of your life to seek your own pleasure and escape from what is disagreeable, calamity might come just the same; and it would be calamity falling on a base mind, which is the one form of sorrow that has no balm in it, and that may well make a man say, "It would have been better for me if I had never been born." I will tell you something, Lillo.'

"Romola paused for a moment. She had taken Lillo's cheeks between her hands, and his young eyes were meeting hers.

" 'There was a man to whom I was very near, so that I could see a great deal of his life, who made almost every one fond of him, for he was young, and clever, and beautiful, and his manners to all were gentle and kind. I believe, when I first knew him, he never thought of anything cruel or base. But because he tried to slip away from everything that was unpleasant, and cared for nothing else so much as his own safety, he came at last to commit some of the basest deeds—such as make men infamous. He denied his father, and left him to misery; he betrayed every trust that was reposed in him, that he might keep himself safe and get rich and prosperous. Yet calamity overtook him.'

"Again Romola paused. Her voice was unsteady, and Lillo was looking up at her with awed wonder.

" 'Another time, my Lillo—I will tell you another time. See, there are our old Piero di Cosimo and Nello coming up the Borgo Pinti, bringing us their flowers. Let us go and wave our hands to them, that they may know we see them.' "

Hardly one of George Eliot's stories has a conventional "happy ending." Yet they leave us not depressed, but strengthened to endure and invigorated to endeavour. In this they differ absolutely from the pessimistic novels of the present hour, which not only leave a bad taste in the mouth, but also a sense of futility in the heart.

Let me turn now to her first two novels, which still seem to me her best. Bear in mind, I am not formulating academic theories, nor pronouncing *ex cathedrâ* judgments, but simply recording for the consideration of other readers certain personal observations and reactions.

Adam Bede is a novel of rustic tragedy in which some of the characters are drawn directly from memory. Adam is a partial portrait of George Eliot's father, and Dinah Morris a sketch of her aunt, a Methodist woman preacher. There is plenty of comic relief in the story, admirably done.

Take the tongue duel between Bartle Massey, the sharp-spoken, kind-hearted bachelor schoolmaster, and Mrs. Poyser, the humorous, pungent, motherly wife of the old farmer.

" 'What!' said Bartle, with an air of disgust. 'Was there a woman concerned? Then I give you up, Adam.'

" 'But it's a woman you'n spoke well on, Bartle,' said Mr. Poyser. 'Come, now, you canna draw back; you said once as women wouldna ha' been a bad invention if they'd all been like Dinah.'

" 'I meant her voice, man—I meant her voice, that was all,' said Bartle. 'I can bear to hear her speak without wanting to put wool in my ears. As for other things, I dare say she's like the rest o' the women—thinks two and two 'ull come to make five, if she cries and bothers enough about it.'

" 'Ay, ay!' said Mrs. Poyser; 'one 'ud think, an' hear some folks talk, as the men war 'cute enough to count the corns in a bag o' wheat wi' only smelling at it. They can see through a barn door, *they* can. Perhaps that's the reason they can see so little o' this side on't.'

" 'Ah!' said Bartle, sneeringly, 'the women are

quick enough—they're quick enough. They know the rights of a story before they hear it, and can tell a man what his thoughts are before he knows 'em himself.'

" 'Like enough,' said Mrs. Poyser; 'for the men are mostly so slow, their thoughts overrun 'em, an' they can only catch 'em by the tail. I can count a stocking-top while a man's getting's tongue ready; an' when he outs wi' his speech at last, there's little broth to be made on't. It's your dead chicks take the longest hatchin'. Howiver, I'm not denyin' the women are foolish: God Almighty made 'em to match the men.'

" 'Match!' said Bartle; 'ay, as vinegar matches one's teeth. If a man says a word, his wife 'll match it with a contradiction; if he's a mind for hot meat, his wife 'll match it with cold bacon; if he laughs, she'll match him with whimpering. She's such a match as the horsefly is to th' horse: she's got the right venom to sting him with—the right venom to sting him with.'

" 'What dost say to that?' said Mr. Poyser, throwing himself back and looking merrily at his wife.

" 'Say !' answered Mrs. Poyser, with dangerous fire kindling in her eye; 'why, *I say as some folks' tongues are like the clocks as run on strikin', not to tell you the time o' the day, but because there's summat wrong i' their own inside.'* . . ."

The plot, as in Scott's *Heart of Midlothian*, turns on a case of seduction and child murder, and the contrast between Effie and Jeannie Deans has its parallel in the stronger contrast between Hetty Sorrel and Dinah Morris. Hetty looked as if she were "made of roses"; but she was, in Mrs. Poyser's phrase, "no better nor a cherry wi' a hard stone inside it." Dinah's human beauty of face and voice was the true reflection of her inward life which

> " cast a beam on the outward shape,
> The unpolluted temple of the mind,
> And turned it by degrees to the soul's essence."

The crisis of the book comes in the prison, where Dinah wrestles for the soul of Hetty—a scene as passionate and moving as any in fiction. Dinah triumphs, not by her own might, but by the sheer power and beauty of the Christian faith and love which she embodies.

In George Eliot's novels you will find some passages of stinging and well-merited satire on the semi-pagan, conventional religion of middle-class orthodoxy in England of the nineteenth century—"proud respectability in a gig of unfashionable build; worldliness without side-dishes"—read the chapter on "A Variation of Protestantism Unknown to Bossuet," in *The Mill on the Floss*. But you will not find a single page or paragraph that would draw or drive the reader away from real Christianity. On the contrary, she has expressed the very secret of its appeal to the human heart through the words and conduct of some of her best characters. They do not argue; they utter and show the meaning of religion. On me the effect of her books is a deepened sense of the inevitable need of Christ and his gospel to sustain and nourish the high morality of courage and compassion, patience, and hope, which she so faithfully teaches.

The truth is, George Eliot lived in the afterglow of Christian faith. Rare souls are capable of doing that. But mankind at large needs the sunrise.

The Mill on the Floss is partly an autobiographic

romance. Maggie Tulliver's character resembles George Eliot in her youth. The contrast between the practical and the ideal, the conflict between love and duty in the heart of a girl, belong to those *problematische Naturen*, as Goethe called them, which may taste keen joys but cannot escape sharp sorrows. The centre of the story lies in Maggie's strong devotion to her father and to her brother Tom—a person not altogether unlike the "elder brother" in the parable—in strife with her love for Philip, the son of the family enemy. Tom ruthlessly commands his sister to choose between breaking with him and giving up her lover. Maggie, after a bitter struggle, chooses her brother. Would a real woman do that? Yes, I have known some very real women who have done it, in one case with a tragic result.

The original title of this book (and the right one) was *Sister Maggie*. Yet we can see why George Eliot chose the other name. The little river Floss, so tranquil in its regular tidal flow, yet capable of such fierce and sudden outbreaks, runs through the book from beginning to end. It is a mysterious type of the ineluctable power of Nature in man's mortal drama.

In the last chapter, when the flood comes, and the erring sister who loved her brother so tenderly, rescues him who loved her so cruelly from the ruined mill, the frail skiff which carries them clasped heart to heart, reconciled in that revealing moment, goes down in the senseless irresistible rush of waters.

It is not a "bad ending." The sister's love triumphs. Such a close was inevitable for such a story. But it is not a conclusion. It cries out for immortality.

On the art of George Eliot judgments have differed. Mr. Oscar Browning, a respectable authority, thinks highly of it. Mr. W. C. Brownell, a far better critic, indeed one of the very best, thinks less favourably of it, says that it is too intellectual; that the development and conduct of her characters are too logical and consistent; that the element of surprize, which is always present in life, is lacking in her people. "Our attention," he writes, "is so concentrated on what they think that we hardly know how they feel, or whether . . . they feel at all." This criticism does not seem to me altogether just. Certainly there is no lack of surprize in Maggie Tulliver's temporary infatuation with the handsome, light-minded Stephen Guest, or in Dorothea Brooke's marriage to that heady young butterfly, Will Ladislaw. These things certainly were not arrived at by logical consistency. Nor can one lay his hand on his heart and say that there is no feeling in the chapter where the fugitive Romola comes as Madonna to the mountain village, stricken by pestilence, or in the passage where Dinah Morris strives for Hetty's soul in prison.

George Eliot herself tells us the purpose of her art—it is *verity*.

"It is for this rare, precious quality of truthfulness that I delight in many Dutch paintings, which lofty-minded people despise. . . . All honour and reverence to the divine beauty of form! Let us cultivate it to the utmost in men, women, and children—in our gardens and in our homes. But let us love that other beauty, too, which lies in no secret of proportion, but in the secret of deep human sympathy."

It is Rembrandt, then, rather than Titian, who

is her chosen painter. But she does not often attain his marvellous *chiaroscuro*.

Her style is clear and almost always firm in drawing, though deficient in colour. It is full of meaning, almost over-scrupulous in defining precisely what she wishes to express. Here and there it flashes into a wise saying, a sparkling epigram. At other times, especially in her later books, it spreads out and becomes too diffuse, too slow, like Sir Walter Scott's. But it never repels by vulgar smartness, nor perplexes by vagueness and artificial obscurity. It serves her purpose well—to convey the results of her scrutiny of the inner life and her loving observation of the outer life in its humblest forms. In these respects it is admirable and satisfying. And it is her own—she does not imitate, nor write according to a theory.

Her general view of human nature is not essentially different from that expressed in a passage which I quoted from Thackeray in the previous chapter. We are none of us "irreproachable characters." We are "mixed human beings." Therefore she wishes to tell her stories "in such a way as to call forth tolerant judgment, pity, and sympathy."

As I began so let me end this chapter—with a word on women. For myself, I think it wise and prudent to maintain with Plutarch that *virtue* in man and woman is one and the same. Yet there is a difference between the feminine and the masculine virtues. This opinion Plutarch sets forth and illustrates in his brief histories, and George Eliot in her novels. But of the virtues of women she gives more and finer examples.

THE POET OF IMMORTAL
YOUTH

THE POET OF IMMORTAL
YOUTH

ONE of the things that surprized and bewildered old Colonel Newcome when he gathered his boy's friends around the mahogany tree in the dull, respectable dining-room at 12 Fitzroy Square, was to hear George Warrington declare, between huge puffs of tobacco smoke, "that young Keats was a genius to be estimated in future days with young Raphael." At this Charles Honeyman sagely nodded his ambrosial head, while Clive Newcome assented with sparkling eyes. But to the Colonel, sitting kindly grave and silent at the head of the table, and recalling (somewhat dimly) the bewigged and powdered poetry of the age of Queen Anne, such a critical sentiment seemed radical and revolutionary, almost ungentlemanly.

How astonished he would have been sixty years later if he had taken up Mr. Sidney Colvin's *Life of Keats*, in the "English Men of Letters Series," and read in the concluding chapter the deliberate and remarkable judgment that "by power, as well as by temperament and aim, he was the most Shakespearean spirit that has lived since Shakespeare"!

In truth, from the beginning the poetry of Keats has been visited too much by thunder-storms of praise. It was the indiscriminate enthusiasm of his friends that drew out the equally indiscriminate ridicule of his enemies. It was the premature salutation offered to him as a supreme master of the most difficult of all arts that gave point and sting to the criticism of evident defects in his work. *The Examiner* hailed him, before his first volume had been printed, as one who was destined to revive the early vigour of English poetry. *Blackwood's Magazine* retorted by quoting his feeblest lines and calling him "Johnny Keats." The suspicion of log-rolling led to its usual result in a volley of stone-throwing.

Happily, the ultimate fame and influence of a true poet are not determined by the partizan conflicts which are waged about his name. He may suffer some personal loss by having to breathe, at times, a perturbed atmosphere of mingled flattery and abuse instead of the still air of delightful studies. He may be robbed of some days of a life already far too short, by the pestilent noise and confusion arising from that scramble for notoriety which is often unduly honoured with the name of "literary activity." And there are some men whose days of real inspiration are so few, and whose poetic gift is so slender, that this loss proves fatal to them. They are completely carried away and absorbed by the speculations and strifes of the market-place. They spend their time in the intrigues of rival poetic enterprises, and learn to regard current quotations in the trade journals as the only standard of value. Minor poets at the outset, they are tempted to risk their little all on the stock exchange of literature, and, losing their last title to the noun, retire to bankruptcy on the adjective.

But Keats did not belong to this frail and foolish race. His lot was cast in a world of petty conflict and ungenerous rivalry, but he was not of that world. It hurt him a little, but it did not ruin him. His spiritual capital was too large, and he regarded it as too sacred to be imperilled by vain speculations.

169

He had in Chaucer and Spenser, Shakespeare and
Chapman, Milton and Petrarch, older and wiser
friends than Leigh Hunt. For him

> "The blue
> Bared its eternal bosom, and the dew
> Of summer nights collected still to make
> The morning precious: beauty was awake!"

He perceived, by that light which comes only to
high-souled and noble-hearted poets,

> "The great end
> Of poesy, that it should be a friend
> To soothe the cares and lift the thoughts of man."

To that end he gave the best that he had to give,
freely, generously, joyously pouring himself into
the ministry of his art. He did not dream for a
moment that the gift was perfect. Flattery could
not blind him to the limitations and defects of his
early work. He was his own best and clearest critic.
But he knew that so far as it went his poetic inspiration was true. He had faithfully followed the
light of a pure and elevating joy in the opulent,
manifold beauty of nature and in the eloquent significance of old-world legends, and he believed that

170

it had already led him to a place among the poets whose verse would bring delight, in far-off years, to the sons and daughters of mankind. He believed also that if he kept alive his faith in the truth of beauty and the beauty of truth it would lead him on yet further, into a nobler life and closer to those immortal bards whose

> "Souls still speak
> To mortals of their little week;
> Of their sorrows and delights;
> Of their passions and their spites;
> Of their glory and their shame;
> What doth strengthen and what maim."

He expressed this faith very clearly in the early and uneven poem called "Sleep and Poetry," in a passage which begins

> "Oh, for ten years, that I may overwhelm
> Myself in poesy! so I may do the deed
> That my own soul has to itself decreed."

And then, ere four years had followed that brave wish, his voice fell silent under a wasting agony of pain and love, and the daisies were growing upon his Roman grave.

The pathos of his frustrated hope, his early death,

has sometimes blinded men a little, it seems to me, to the real significance of his work and the true quality of his influence in poetry. He has been lamented in the golden verse of Shelley's "Adonaïs," and in the prose of a hundred writers who have shared Shelley's error without partaking of his genius, as the loveliest innocent ever martyred by the cruelty of hostile critics. But, in fact, the vituperations of Gifford and his crew were no more responsible for the death of Keats, than the stings of insects are for the death of a man who has perished of hunger on the coast of Labrador. They added to his sufferings, no doubt, but they did not take away his life. Keats had far too much virtue in the old Roman sense—far too much courage, to be killed by a criticism. He died of consumption, as he clearly and sadly knew that he was fated to do when he first saw the drop of arterial blood upon his pillow.

Nor is it just, although it may seem generous, to estimate his fame chiefly by the anticipation of what he might have accomplished if he had lived longer; to praise him for his promise at the expense of his performance; and to rest his claim to a place among the English poets upon an uncertain prophecy of rivalry with Shakespeare. I find a far sounder note in Lowell's manly essay, when he says: "No doubt there is something tropical and of strange overgrowth in his sudden maturity, but it *was* maturity nevertheless." I hear the accent of a wiser and saner criticism in the sonnet of one of our American poets:

"Touch not with dark regret his perfect fame,
    Sighing, 'Had he but lived he had done so';
    Or, 'Were his heart not eaten out with woe
John Keats had won a prouder, mightier name!'
Take him for what he was and did—nor blame
    Blind fate for all he suffered. Thou shouldst know
    Souls such as his escape no mortal blow—
No agony of joy, or sorrow, or shame."

.   .   .   .

"Take him for what he was and did"—that should be the key-note of our thought of Keats as a poet. The exquisite harmony of his actual work with his actual character; the truth of what he wrote to what his young heart saw and felt and enjoyed; the simplicity of his very exuberance of

173

ornament, and the naturalness of his artifice; the sincerity of his love of beauty and the beauty of his sincerity—these are the qualities which give an individual and lasting charm to his poetry, and make his gift to the world complete in itself and very precious, although,—or perhaps we should even say because,—it was unfinished.

Youth itself is imperfect: it is impulsive, visionary, and unrestrained; full of tremulous delight in its sensations, but not yet thoroughly awake to the deeper meanings of the world; avid of novelty and mystery, but not yet fully capable of hearing or interpreting the still, small voice of divine significance which breathes from the simple and familiar elements of life.

Yet youth has its own completeness as a season of man's existence. It is justified and indispensable. Alfred de Musset's

"We old men born yesterday"

are simply monstrous. The poetry which expresses and represents youth, the poetry of sensation and sentiment, has its own place in the literature of the world. This is the order to which the poetry of Keats belongs.

He is not a feminine poet, as Mr. Coventry Patmore calls him, any more than Theocritus or Tennyson is feminine; for the quality of extreme sensitiveness to outward beauty is not a mark of femininity. It is found in men more often and more clearly than in women. But it is always most keen and joyous and overmastering in the morning of the soul.

Keats is not a virile poet, like Dante or Shakespeare or Milton; that he would have become one if he had lived is a happy and loving guess. He is certainly not a member of the senile school of poetry, which celebrates the impotent and morbid passions of decay, with a *café chantant* for its temple, and the smoke of cigarettes for incense, and cups of absinthe for its libations, and for its goddess not the immortal Venus rising from the sea, but the weary, painted, and decrepit Venus sinking into the gutter.

He is in the highest and best sense of the word a juvenile poet—"mature," as Lowell says, but

mature, as genius always is, within the boundaries
and in the spirit of his own season of life. The very
sadness of his lovely odes, "To a Nightingale,"
"On a Grecian Urn," "To Autumn," "To Psyche,"
is the pleasant melancholy of the springtime of the
heart. "The Eve of St. Agnes," pure and passionate, surprizing us by its fine excess of colour and
melody, sensuous in every line, yet free from the
slightest taint of sensuality, is unforgetable and
unsurpassable as the dream of first love. The poetry
of Keats, small in bulk and slight in body as it seems
at first sight to be, endures, and will endure, in English literature, because it is the embodiment of *the
spirit of immortal youth*.

Here, I think, we touch its secret as an influence
upon other poets. For that it has been an influence,
—in the older sense of the word, which carries with
it a reference to the guiding and controlling force
supposed to flow from the stars to the earth,—is beyond all doubt. The *History of English Literature*,
with which Taine amused us some fifty years ago,
nowhere displays its narrowness of vision more egre-
giously than in its failure to take account of Gray,

Collins, and Keats as fashioners of English poetry. It does not mention Gray and Collins at all; the name of Keats occurs only once, with a reference to "sickly or overflowing imagination," but to Byron nearly fifty pages are devoted. The American critic, Stedman, showed a far broader and more intelligent understanding of the subject when he said that "Wordsworth begot the mind, and Keats the body, of the idyllic Victorian School."

We can trace the influence of Keats not merely in the conscious or unconscious imitations of his manner, like those which are so evident in the early poems of Tennyson and Procter, in Hood's *Plea of the Midsummer Fairies* and *Lycus the Centaur*, in Rossetti's *Ballads and Sonnets*, and William Morris's *Earthly Paradise*, but also in the youthful spirit of delight in the retelling of old tales of mythology and chivalry; in the quickened sense of pleasure in the luxuriance and abundance of natural beauty; in the freedom of overflowing cadences transmuting ancient forms of verse into new and more flexible measures; in the large liberty of imaginative diction, making all nature sympathize with the joy and sorrow of man,—in brief, in many of the finest marks of a renascence, a renewed youth, which characterize the poetry of the early Victorian era.

I do not mean to say that Keats alone, or chiefly, was responsible for this renascence. He never set up to lead a movement or to found a school. His genius is not to be compared to that of a commanding artist like Giotto or Leonardo or Michelagnolo, but rather to that of a painter like Botticelli, whose personal and expressive charm makes itself felt in the work of many painters, who learned secrets of grace and beauty from him, though they were not his professed disciples or followers.

Take for example Matthew Arnold. He called himself, and no doubt rightly, a Wordsworthian. But it was not from Wordsworth that he caught the strange and searching melody of "The Forsaken Merman," or learned to embroider the laments for "Thyrsis" and "The Scholar-Gypsy" with such opulence of varied bloom as makes death itself seem lovely. It was from John Keats. Or read the description of the tapestry on the castle walls in "Tristram and Iseult." How perfectly that repeats the spirit of Keats's descriptions in "The Eve of St. Agnes"! It is the poetry of the picturesque.

Indeed, we shall fail to do justice to the influence of Keats unless we recognize also that it has produced direct and distinct effects in the art of painting. The English pre-Raphaelites owed much to his inspiration. Holman Hunt found two of his earliest subjects for pictures in "The Eve of St. Agnes" and "The Pot of Basil." Millais painted "Lorenzo and Isabella," and Rossetti "La Belle Dame sans Merci." There is an evident sympathy between the art of these painters, which insisted that every detail in a picture is precious and should be painted with truthful care for its beauty, and the poetry of Keats, which is filled, and even overfilled, with minute and loving touches of exquisite elaboration.

But it must be remembered that in poetry, as well as in painting, the spirit of picturesqueness has its dangers. The details may be multiplied until the original design is lost. The harmony and lucidity of a poem may be destroyed by innumerable digressions and descriptions. In some of his

poems—in "Endymion" and in "Lamia"—Keats
fell very deep into this fault, and no one knew it
better than himself. But when he was at his best
he had the power of adding a hundred delicate details to his central vision, and making every touch
heighten and enhance the general effect. How
wonderful in its unity is the "Ode on a Grecian
Urn"! How completely magical are the opening
lines of "Hyperion":

> "Deep in the shady sadness of a vale
> Far sunken from the healthy breath of morn,
> Far from the fiery Noon, and eve's one star,
> Sat gray-hair'd Saturn, quiet as a stone,
> Still as the silence round about his lair;
> Forest on forest hung about his head
> Like cloud on cloud."

How large and splendid is the imagery of the sonnet "On First Looking into Chapman's Homer"!
And who that has any sense of poetry does not recognize the voice of a young master in the two superb
lines of the last poem that Keats wrote?—the sonnet in which he speaks of the bright star

> "watching, with eternal lids apart,
> Like Nature's patient, sleepless Eremite,

The moving waters at their priestlike task
Of pure ablution round earth's human shores."

The poets of America have not been slow to recognize the charm and power of Keats. Holmes and Longfellow and Lowell paid homage to him in their verse. Lanier inscribed to his memory a poem called "Clover." Gilder wrote two sonnets which celebrate his "perfect fame." Robert Underwood Johnson has a lovely lyric on "The Name Writ in Water."

But I find an even deeper and larger tribute to his influence in the features of resemblance to his manner and spirit which flash out here and there, unexpectedly and unconsciously, in the poetry of our New World. Emerson was so unlike Keats in his intellectual constitution as to make all contact between them appear improbable, if not impossible. Yet no one can read Emerson's "May-Day," and Keats' exquisitely truthful and imaginative lines on "Fancy," one after the other, without feeling that the two poems are very near of kin. Lowell's "Legend of Brittany" has caught, not only the measure, but also the tone and the diction of "Isabella." The famous introduction to "The Vision of Sir Launfal," with its often quoted line,

> "What is so rare as a day in June?"

finds a parallel in the opening verses of "Sleep and Poetry"—

> "What is more gentle than a wind in summer?"

Lowell's "Endymion," which he calls "a mystical comment on Titian's 'Sacred and Profane Love,'" is full of echoes from Keats, like this:

> "My day began not till the twilight fell
> And lo! in ether from heaven's sweetest well
> The new moon swam, divinely isolate
> In maiden silence, she that makes my fate
> Haply not knowing it, or only so
> As I the secrets of my sheep may know."

In Lanier's rich and melodious "Hymns of the Marshes" there are innumerable touches in the style of Keats; for example, his apostrophe to the

> "Reverend marsh, low-couched along the sea,
> Old chemist, wrapped in alchemy,
> Distilling silence,——"

or his praise of the

> "Beautiful glooms, soft dusks in the noon-day fire,
> Wildwood privacies, closets of lone desire,

Chamber from chamber parted with wavering arras of
leaves."

One of the finest pieces of elegiac verse that have
yet been produced in America, George E. Woodberry's poem called "The North Shore Watch," has
many passages that recall the young poet who wrote

"A thing of beauty is a joy forever."

Indeed, we hear the very spirit of Endymion speaking in Woodberry's lines:

"Beauty abides, nor suffers mortal change,
Eternal refuge of the orphaned mind."

Father John B. Tabb, who had the exquisite art of
the Greek epigram at his command, in one of his
delicately finished little poems, imagined Sappho
listening to the "Ode to a Nightingale":

"Methinks when first the nightingale
Was mated to thy deathless song,
That Sappho with emotion pale
Amid the Olympian throng,
Again, as in the Lesbian grove,
Stood listening with lips apart,
To hear in thy melodious love
The pantings of her heart."

Yes; the memory and influence of Keats endure, and will endure, because his poetry expresses something in the heart that will not die so long as there are young men and maidens to see and feel the beauty of the world and the thrill of love. His poetry is complete, it is true, it is justified, because it is the fitting utterance of one of those periods of mental life which Keats himself has called "the human seasons."

But its completeness and its truth depend upon its relation, in itself and in the poet's mind, to the larger world of poetry, the fuller life, the rounded year of man. Nor was this forward look, this anticipation of something better and greater yet to come, lacking in the youth of Keats. It flashes out, again and again, from his letters, those outpourings of his heart and mind, so full of boyish exuberance and manly vigour, so rich in revelations of what this marvellous, beautiful, sensitive, courageous little creature really was,—a great soul in the body of a lad. It shows itself clearly and calmly in the remarkable preface in which he criticizes his own "Endymion," calling it "a feverish attempt, rather than a deed accomplished." "It is just," he writes, "that this youngster should die away: a sad thought for me, if I had not some hope that while it is dwindling I may be plotting, and fitting myself for verses fit to live." The same fine hope of a sane and manly youth is expressed in his early verses entitled "Sleep and Poetry." He has been speaking of the first joys of his fancy, in the realm of Flora and old Pan: the merry games and dances with white-handed nymphs: the ardent pursuit of love, and the satisfied repose in the bosom of a leafy world. Then his imagination goes on to something better.

"And can I ever bid these joys farewell?
Yes, I must pass them for a nobler life,
Where I may find the agonies, the strife
Of human hearts: for lo! I see afar,
O'ersailing the blue cragginess, a car
And steeds with streamy manes—the charioteer
Looks out upon the winds with glorious fear:
And now the numerous tramplings quiver lightly
Along a huge cloud's ridge: and now with sprightly
Wheel downward come they into fresher skies,
Tipt round with silver from the sun's bright eyes.
            . . . And there soon appear
Shapes of delight, of mystery and fear,
Passing along before a dusky space

185

Made by some mighty oaks: as they would chase
Some ever-fleeting music, on they sweep.
Lo! how they murmur, laugh, and smile, and weep:
Some with upholden hand and mouth severe;
Some with their faces muffled to the ear
Between their arms; some, clear in youthful bloom,
Go glad and smilingly across the gloom;
Some looking back, and some with upward gaze;
Yes, thousands in a thousand different ways
Flit onward—now a lovely wreath of girls
Dancing their sleek hair into tangled curls;
And now broad wings.   Most awfully intent
The driver of those steeds is forward bent,
And seems to listen: O that I might know
All that he writes with such a hurrying glow.

The visions all are fled—the car is fled
Into the light of heaven, and in their stead
A sense of real things comes doubly strong,
And, like a muddy stream, would bear along
My soul to nothingness: but I will strive
Against all doubtings, and will keep alive
The thought of that same chariot, and the strange
Journey it went."

How young-hearted is this vision, how full of
thronging fancies and half-apprehended mystic
meanings! Yet how unmistakably it has the long,
high, forward look toward manhood, without which
youth itself is not rounded and complete!

186

After all, that look, that brave expectation, is vital in our picture of Keats. It is one of the reasons why we love him. It is one of the things which make his slender volume of poetry so companionable, even as an ardent, dreamy man is doubly a good comrade when we feel in him the hope of a strong man. We cannot truly understand the wonderful performance of Keats without considering his promise; we cannot appreciate what he did without remembering that it was only part of what he hoped to do.

He was not one of those who believe that the ultimate aim of poetry is sensuous loveliness, and that there is no higher law above the law of "art for art's sake." The poets of arrested development, the artificers of mere melody and form, who say that art must always play and never teach, the musicians who are content to remain forever

> "The idle singers of an empty day,"

are not his true followers.

He held that "beauty is truth." But he held also another article that has been too often left out in the repetition of his poetic creed: he held "truth, beauty," and he hoped one day to give a clear, full utterance to that higher, holier vision. Perhaps he has, but not to mortal ears.

THE RECOVERY OF JOY

THE RECOVERY OF JOY

WORDSWORTH'S POETRY

WHEN this essay was written, a good many years ago, there was no available biography of Wordsworth except the two-volume *Memoir* by Bishop Christopher Wordsworth, the poet's nephew. It is a solid work of family piety, admiring and admirable; but it must be admitted that it is dull. It is full of matters of no particular consequence, and it leaves out events in the poet's life and traits in his character which are not only interesting in themselves but also of real importance to a vital understanding of his work.

Even while reading the *Memoir*, I felt sure that he was not always the tranquil, patient, wise, serenely happy sage that he appeared in his later years,—sure that a joy in peace as deep and strong as his was, could only have been won through sharp conflict,—sure that the smooth portrait drawn by the reverent hand of the bishop did not fully and frankly depict the real man who wrote the deep and moving poetry of Wordsworth.

It was about this time that the valuable studies of Wordsworth's early life which had been made by Professor Emile Legouis, (then of the University of Lyons, now of the Sorbonne,) were published in English. This volume threw a new light upon the poet's nature, revealing its intense, romantic strain, and making clear at least some of the causes which led to the shipwreck of his first hopes and to the period of profound gloom which followed his return from residence in France in December 1792.

Shortly after reading Professor Legouis' book, I met by chance a gentleman in Baltimore and was convinced by what he told me, (in a conversation which I do not feel at liberty to repeat in detail,) that Wordsworth had a grand "affair of the heart" while he lived in France, with a young French lady of excellent family and character. But they were parted. A daughter was born, (whom he legitimated according to French law,) and descendants of that daughter were living.

There was therefore solid ground for my feeling

that the poet was not a man who had been always and easily decorous. He had passed through a time of storm and stress. He had lost not only his political dreams and his hopes of a career, but also his first love and his joy. The knowledge of this gave his poetry a new meaning for me, brought it nearer, made it seem more deeply human. It was under the influence of this feeling that this essay was written in a farmhouse in Tyringham Valley, where I was staying in the winter of 1897, with Richard Watson Gilder and his wife.

Since then Professor George McLean Harper has completed and published, (1916,) his classic book on *William Wordsworth, His Life, Works, and Influence*. This is undoubtedly the very best biography of the poet, and it contains much new material, particularly with reference to his life and connections in France. But there is nothing in it to shake, and on the contrary there is much to confirm, the opinion which was first put forth in this essay: namely, that the central theme, the great significance, of Wordsworth's poetry is *the recovery of joy*.

I

William Wordsworth was born in 1770 in the town of Cockermouth in Cumberland; educated in the village school of Hawkshead among the mountains, and at St. John's College, Cambridge. A dreamy, moody youth; always ambitious, but not always industrious; passionate in disposition, with high spirits, simple tastes, and independent virtues; he did not win, and seems not to have desired, university honours. His principal property when he came of age consisted of two manuscript poems,— *An Evening Walk* and *Descriptive Sketches,*—composed in the manner of Cowper's *Task.* With these in his pocket he wandered over to France; partly to study the language; partly to indulge his inborn love of travel by a second journey on the Continent; and partly to look on at the vivid scenes of the French Revolution. But the vast dæmonic movement of which he proposed to be a spectator caught his mind in its current and swept him out of his former self.

Wordsworth was not originally a revolutionist,

like Coleridge and Southey. He was not even a
native radical, except as all simplicity and austerity
of character tend towards radicalism. When he
passed through Paris, in November of 1791, and
picked up a bit of stone from the ruins of the Bas-
tile as a souvenir, it was only a sign of youthful
sentimentality. But when he came back to Paris
in October of 1792, after a winter at Orleans and a
summer at Blois, in close intercourse with that
ardent and noble republican, Michael Beaupuy,
he had been converted into an eager partisan of the
Republic. He even dreamed of throwing himself
into the conflict, reflecting on "the power of one
pure and energetic will to accomplish great things."

His conversion was not, it seems to me, primarily
a matter of intellectual conviction. It was an affair
of emotional sympathy. His knowledge of the
political and social theories of the Revolution was
but superficial. He was never a doctrinaire. The
influence of Rousseau and Condorcet did not penetrate far beneath the skin of his mind. It was the
primal joy of the Revolutionary movement that
fascinated him,—the confused glimmering of new

hopes and aspirations for mankind. He was like a man who has journeyed, half asleep, from the frost-bound dulness of a wintry clime, and finds himself, fully awake, in a new country, where the time for the singing of birds has come, and the multitudinous blossoming of spring bursts forth. He is possessed by the spirit of joy, and reason follows where feeling leads the way. Wordsworth himself has confessed, half unconsciously, the secret of his conversion in his lines on *The French Revolution as it appeared to Enthusiasts at its Commencement.*

> "Oh! pleasant exercise of hope and joy!
> For mighty were the auxiliars which then stood
> Upon our side, we who were strong in love!
> Bliss was it in that dawn to be alive,
> But to be young was very heaven!"

There was another "bliss," keener even than the dreams of political enthusiasm, that thrilled him in this momentous year,—the rapture of romantic love. Into this he threw himself with ardour and tasted all its joy. We do not know exactly what it was that broke the vision and dashed the cup of gladness from his lips. Perhaps it was some difficulty with the girl's family, who were royalists.

Perhaps it was simply the poet's poverty. Whatever the cause was, love's young dream was shattered, and there was nothing left but the painful memory of an error, to be atoned for in later years as best he could.

His political hopes and ideals were darkened by the actual horrors which filled Paris during the fall of 1792. His impulse to become a revolutionist was shaken, if not altogether broken. Returning to England at the end of the same year, he tried to sustain his sinking spirits by setting in order the reasons and grounds of his new-born enthusiasm, already waning. His letter to Bishop Watson, written in 1793, is the fullest statement of republican sympathies that he ever made. In it he even seems to justify the execution of Louis XVI, and makes light of "the idle cry of modish lamentation which has resounded from the court to the cottage" over the royal martyr's fate. He defends the right of the people to overthrow all who oppress them, to choose their own rulers, to direct their own destiny by universal suffrage, and to sweep all obstacles out of their way. The reasoning is so absolute, so relentless, the scorn for all who oppose it is so lofty, that already we begin to suspect a wavering conviction intrenching itself for safety.

The course of events in France was ill fitted to nourish the joy of a pure-minded enthusiast. The tumultuous terrors of the Revolution trod its ideals in the dust. Its light was obscured in its own sulphurous smoke. Robespierre ran his bloody course to the end; and when his head fell under the guillotine, Wordsworth could not but exult. War was declared between France and England, and his heart was divided; but the deeper and stronger ties were those that bound him to his own country. He was English in his very flesh and bones. The framework of his mind was of Cumberland. So he stood rooted in his native allegiance, while the leaves and blossoms of joy fell from him, like a tree stripped bare by the first great gale of autumn.

The years from 1793 to 1795 were the period of his deepest poverty, spiritual and material. His youthful poems, published in 1793, met with no more success than they deserved. His plans for entering into active life were feeble and futile. His mind was darkened and confused, his faith shaken to the foundation, and his feelings clouded with despair. In this crisis of disaster two gifts of fortune came to him. His sister Dorothy took her place at his side, to lead him back by her wise, tender, cheerful love from the far country of despair. His friend Raisley Calvert bequeathed to him a legacy of nine hundred pounds; a small inheritance, but enough to protect him from the wolf of poverty, while he devoted his life to the muse. From the autumn of 1795, when he and his sister set up housekeeping together in a farmhouse at Racedown, until his death in 1850 in the cottage at Rydal Mount, where he had lived for thirty-seven years with his wife and children, there was never any doubt about the disposition of his life. It was wholly dedicated to poetry.

II

But what kind of poetry? What was to be its motive power? What its animating spirit? Here the experience of life acting upon his natural character became the deciding factor.

Wordsworth was born a lover of joy, not sensual,

but spiritual. The first thing that happened to him, when he went out into the world, was that he went bankrupt of joy. The enthusiasm of his youth was dashed, the high hope of his spirit was quenched. At the touch of reality his dreams dissolved. It seemed as though he were altogether beaten, a broken man. But with the gentle courage of his sister to sustain him, his indomitable spirit rose again, to renew the adventure of life. He did not evade the issue, by turning aside to seek for fame or wealth. His problem from first to last was the problem of joy,—inward, sincere, imperishable joy. How to recover it after life's disappointments, how to deepen it amid life's illusions, how to secure it through life's trials, how to spread it among life's confusions,—this was the problem that he faced. This was the wealth that he desired to possess, and to increase, and to diffuse,—the wealth

"Of joy in widest commonalty spread."

None of the poets has been as clear as Wordsworth in the avowal that the immediate end of poetry is pleasure. "We have no sympathy," said he, "but what is propagated by pleasure, . . . wherever

After an engraving by J. Bromley.

WILLIAM WORDSWORTH.
Painted by W. Boxall.

we sympathise with pain, it will be found that the sympathy is produced and carried on by subtle combinations with pleasure. We have no knowledge, that is no general principles drawn from the contemplation of particular facts, but what has been built up by pleasure, and exists in us by pleasure alone." And again: "The end of Poetry is to produce excitement, in co-existence with an over-balance of pleasure."

But it may be clearly read in his poetry that what he means by "pleasure" is really an inward, spiritual joy. It is such a joy, in its various forms, that charms him most as he sees it in the world. His gallery of human portraits contains many figures, but every one of them is presented in the light of joy,—the rising light of dawn, or the waning light of sunset. *Lucy Gray* and the little maid in *We are Seven* are childish shapes of joy. The *Highland Girl* is an embodiment of virginal gladness, and the poet cries

> " Now thanks to Heaven! that of its grace
> Hath led me to this lovely place.
> *Joy have I had;* and going hence
> I bear away my recompence."

Wordsworth regards joy as an actual potency of vision:

> " With an eye made quiet by the power
>   Of harmony, and *the deep power of joy*,
>   We see into the heart of things."

Joy is indeed the master-word of his poetry. The dancing daffodils enrich his heart with joy.

> " They flash upon that inward eye
>   Which is the bliss of solitude;
>   And then my heart with pleasure fills,
>   And dances with the daffodils."

The kitten playing with the fallen leaves charms him with pure merriment. The skylark's song lifts him up into the clouds.

> " There is madness about thee, and *joy divine*
>   In that song of thine."

He turns from the nightingale, that creature of a "fiery heart," to the Stock-dove:

> " He sang of love, with quiet blending,
>   Slow to begin and never ending;
>   Of serious faith, *and inward glee;*
>   That was the song—the song for me."

He thinks of love which grows to use

> " *Joy as her holiest language.*"

202

THE RECOVERY OF JOY

He speaks of life's disenchantments and wearinesses
as

> "*All that is at enmity with joy.*"

When autumn closes around him, and the season
makes him conscious that his leaf is sere and yellow
on the bough, he exclaims

> "*Yet will I temperately rejoice;*
> Wide is the range and free the choice
> Of undiscordant themes;
> Which haply kindred souls may prize
> Not less than vernal ecstacies,
> And passion's feverish dreams."

Temperate rejoicing,—that is the clearest note of
Wordsworth's poetry. Not an unrestrained gladness, for he can never escape from that deep, strange
experience of his youth. Often, in thought, he

> "Must hear Humanity in fields and groves
> Pipe solitary anguish; or must hang
> Brooding above the fierce confederate storm
> Of sorrow, barricadoed evermore
> Within the walls of cities."

But even while he hears these sounds he will not be
"downcast or forlorn." He will find a deeper music

to conquer these clashing discords. He will learn, and teach, a hidden joy, strong to survive amid the sorrows of a world like this. He will not look for it in some far-off unrealized Utopia,

> " But in the very world which is the world
> Of all of us,—*the place where in the end*
> *We find our happiness, or not at all!* "

To this quest of joy, to this proclamation of joy, he dedicates his life.

> " By words
> Which speak of nothing more than what we are
> Would I arouse the sensual from their sleep
> Of Death, and win the vacant and the vain
> *To noble raptures.*"

And herein he becomes a prophet to his age,—a prophet of the secret of joy, simple, universal, enduring,—the open secret.

The burden of Wordsworth's prophecy of joy, as found in his poetry, is threefold. First, he declares with exultation that he has seen in Nature the evidence of a living spirit in vital correspondence with the spirit of man. Second, he expresses the deepest, tenderest feeling of the inestimable value of the humblest human life,—a feeling which through all its steadiness is yet strangely illumined by sudden gushes of penetration and pathos. Third, he proclaims a lofty ideal of the liberty and greatness of man, consisting in obedience to law and fidelity to duty.

I am careful in choosing words to describe the manner of this threefold prophesying, because I am anxious to distinguish it from didacticism. Not that Wordsworth is never didactic; for he is very often entirely and dreadfully so. But at such times he is not at his best; and it is in these long uninspired intervals that we must bear, as Walter Pater has said, "With patience the presence of an alien element in Wordsworth's work, which never coalesced with what is really delightful in it, nor underwent his peculiar power." Wordsworth's genius as a poet did not always illuminate his industry as a writer. In the intervals he prosed terribly. There is a good deal of what Lowell calls "Dr. Wattsiness," in some of his poems.

But the character of his best poems was strangely inspirational. They came to him like gifts, and he read them aloud as if wondering at their beauty.

Through the protracted description of an excursion, or the careful explanation of a state of mind, he slowly plods on foot; but when he comes to the mount of vision, he mounts up with wings as an eagle. In the analysis of a character, in the narration of a simple story, he often drones, and sometimes stammers; but when the flash of insight arrives, he sings. This is the difference between the pedagogue and the prophet: the pedagogue repeats a lesson learned by rote, the prophet chants a truth revealed by vision.

III

Let me speak first of Wordsworth as a poet of Nature. The peculiar and precious quality of his best work is that it is done with his eye on the object and his imagination beyond it.

Nothing could be more accurate, more true to the facts than Wordsworth's observation of the external world. There was an underlying steadiness, a fundamental placidity, a kind of patient, heroic obstinacy in his character, which blended with his delicate, almost tremulous sensibility, to make him rarely fitted for this work. He could look and listen long. When the magical moment of disclosure arrived, he was there and ready.

Some of his senses were not particularly acute. Odours seem not to have affected him. There are few phrases descriptive of the fragrance of nature in his poetry, and so far as I can remember none of them are vivid. He could never have written Tennyson's line about

"The smell of violets hidden in the green."

Nor was he especially sensitive to colour. Most of his descriptions in this region are vague and luminous, rather than precise and brilliant. Colour-words are comparatively rare in his poems. Yellow, I think, was his favourite, if we may judge by the flowers that he mentioned most frequently. Yet more than any colour he loved clearness, trans-parency, the diaphanous current of a pure stream, the light of sunset

"that imbues
Whate'er it strikes with gem-like hues."

But in two things his power of observation was unsurpassed, I think we may almost say, unrivalled:

in sound, and in movement. For these he had what he describes in his sailor-brother,

> "a watchful heart
> Still couchant, an inevitable ear,
> And an eye practiced like a blind man's touch."

In one of his juvenile poems, a sonnet describing the stillness of the world at twilight, he says:

> "Calm is all nature as a resting wheel;
> The kine are couched upon the dewy grass,
> The horse alone seen dimly as I pass,
> *Is cropping audibly his evening meal.*"

At nightfall, while he is listening to the hooting of the owls and mocking them, there comes an interval of silence, and then

> "a gentle shock of mild surprise
> *Has carried far into his heart the voice
> Of mountain torrents.*"

At midnight, on the summit of Snowdon, from a rift in the cloud-ocean at his feet, he hears

> "the roar of waters, torrents, streams
> Innumerable, roaring with one voice."

Under the shadows of the great yew-trees of Borrowdale he loves

> "To lie and listen to the mountain flood
> *Murmuring from Glaramara's inmost caves.*"

What could be more perfect than the little lyric which begins

> "Yes, it was the mountain echo
> Solitary, clear, profound,
> Answering to the shouting cuckoo
> Giving to her sound for sound."

How poignant is the touch with which he describes the notes of the fiery-hearted Nightingale, singing in the dusk:

> "they pierce and pierce;
> Tumultuous harmony and fierce!"

But at sunrise other choristers make different melodies:

> "The birds are singing in the distant woods;
> Over his own sweet voice the Stock-dove broods;
> The Jay makes answer as the Magpie chatters;
> And all the air is filled with pleasant noise of waters."

Wandering into a lovely glen among the hills, he hears all the voices of nature blending together:

> "The Stream, so ardent in its course before,
> Sent forth such sallies of glad sound that all
> Which I till then had heard, appeared the voice
> Of common pleasure: beast and bird, the lamb,
> The shepherd's dog, the linnet and the thrush

> Vied with this waterfall, and made a song,
> Which while I listened, seemed like the wild growth
> *Or like some natural produce of the air*
> *That could not cease to be.*"

Wordsworth, more than any other English poet, interprets and glorifies the mystery of sound. He is the poet who sits oftenest by the Ear-Gate listening to the whispers and murmurs of the invisible guests who throng that portal into "the city of Man-Soul." Indeed the whole spiritual meaning of nature seems to come to him in the form of sound.

> "Wonder not
> If high the transport, great the joy I felt,
> Communing in this sort through earth and heaven
> With every form of creature, as it looked
> Towards the Uncreated with a countenance
> Of adoration, with an eye of love.
> One song they sang, and it was audible,
> Most audible, then, when the fleshly ear,
> O'ercome by humblest prelude of that strain,
> Forgot her functions and slept undisturbed."

No less wonderful is his sense of the delicate motions of nature, the visible transition of form and outline. How exquisite is the description of a high-poising summer-cloud,

"That heareth not the loud winds when they call;
And moveth all together, if it move at all."

He sees the hazy ridges of the mountains like a golden ladder,

> "Climbing suffused with sunny air
> To stop—no record hath told where!"

He sees the gentle mists

> "Curling with unconfirmed intent
> On that green mountain's side."

He watches the swan swimming on Lake Lucarno,—

> "Behold!—as with a gushing impulse heaves
> That downy prow, and softly cleaves
> The mirror of the crystal flood,
> Vanish inverted hill and shadowy wood."

He catches sight of the fluttering green linnet among the hazel-trees:

> "My dazzled sight he oft deceives,
> A Brother of the dancing leaves."

He looks on the meadows sleeping in the spring sunshine:

> "The cattle are grazing,
> Their heads never raising,
> There are forty feeding like one!"

He beholds the far-off torrent pouring down Ben Cruachan:

> "Yon foaming flood seems motionless as ice;
> Its dizzy turbulence eludes the eye,
> Frozen by distance."

Now in such an observation of Nature as this, so keen, so patient, so loving, so delicate, there is an immediate comfort for the troubled mind, a direct refuge and repose for the heart. To see and hear such things is peace and joy. It is a consolation and an education. Wordsworth himself has said this very distinctly.

> "One impulse from a vernal wood
> May teach you more of man
> Of moral evil and of good
> Than all the sages can."

But the most perfect expression of his faith in the educating power of Nature is given in one of the little group of lyrics which are bound together by the name of Lucy,—love-songs so pure and simple that they seem almost mysterious in their ethereal passion.

> "Three years she grew in sun and shower,
> Then Nature said, 'A lovelier flower

On earth was never sown;
This Child I to myself will take;
She shall be mine, and I will make
    A Lady of my own.

Myself will to my darling be
Both law and impulse; and with me
    The Girl, in rock and plain,
In earth and heaven, in glade and bower,
Shall feel an overseeing power
    To kindle or restrain.

.   .   .   .

The stars of midnight shall be dear
To her; and she shall lean her ear
    In many a secret place
Where rivulets dance their wayward round,
And beauty born of murmuring sound
    Shall pass into her face.'"

The personification of Nature in this poem is at
the farthest removed from the traditional poetic
fiction which peopled the world with Dryads and
Nymphs and Oreads. Nor has it any touch of the
"pathetic fallacy" which imposes the thoughts and
feelings of man upon natural objects. It presents
unconsciously, very simply, and yet prophetically,
Wordsworth's vision of Nature,—a vision whose
distinctive marks are vitality and unity.

213

It is his faith that "every flower enjoys the air it breathes." It is also his faith that underlying and animating all this joy there is the life of one mighty Spirit. This faith rises to its most magnificent expression in the famous *Lines composed a few miles above Tintern Abbey:*

> "And I have felt
> A presence that disturbs me with the joy
> Of elevated thought; a sense sublime
> Of something far more deeply interfused,
> Whose dwelling is the light of setting suns,
> And the round ocean and the living air,
> And the blue sky, and in the mind of man:
> A motion and a spirit, that impels
> All thinking things, all objects of all thought,
> And rolls through all things."

The union of this animating Spirit of Nature, with the beholding, contemplating, rejoicing spirit of man is like a pure and noble marriage, in which man attains peace and the spousal consummation of his being. This is the first remedy which Wordsworth finds for the malady of despair, the first and simplest burden of his prophecy of joy. And he utters it with confidence,

> "Knowing that Nature never did betray
> The heart that loved her; 'tis her privilege,

> Through all the years of this our life, to lead
> From joy to joy: for she can so inform
> The mind that is within us, so impress
> With quietness and beauty, and so feed
> With lofty thoughts, that neither evil tongues,
> Rash judgments, nor the sneers of selfish men,
> Nor greetings where no kindness is, nor all
> The dreary intercourse of daily life,
> Shall e'er prevail against us, or disturb
> Our cheerful faith that all which we behold
> Is full of blessings."

IV

Side by side with this revelation of Nature, and interwoven with it so closely as to be inseparable, Wordsworth was receiving a revelation of humanity, no less marvellous, no less significant for his recovery of joy. Indeed he himself seems to have thought it the more important of the two, for he speaks of the mind of man as

> "My haunt and the main region of my song";

And again he says that he will set out, like an adventurer,

> "And through the human heart explore the way;
> And look and listen—gathering whence I may,
> Triumph, and thoughts no bondage can restrain."

The discovery of humble life, of peasant character, of lowly, trivial scenes and incidents, as a field for poetry, was not original with Wordsworth. But he was the first English poet to explore this field thoroughly, sympathetically, with steady and deepening joy. Burns had been there before him; but the song of Burns though clear and passionate, was fitful. Cowper had been there before him; but Cowper was like a visitor from the polite world, never an inhabitant, never quite able to pierce gently, powerfully down to the realities of lowly life and abide in them. Crabbe had been there before him; but Crabbe was something of a pessimist; he felt the rough shell of the nut, but did not taste the sweet kernel.

Wordsworth, if I may draw a comparison from another art, was the Millet of English poetry. In his verse we find the same quality of perfect comprehension, of tender pathos, of absolute truth interfused with delicate beauty that makes Millet's *Angelus*, and *The Gleaners* and *The Sower* and *The Sheepfold*, immortal visions of the lowly life. Place beside these pictures, if you will, Wordsworth's *Solitary Reaper*, *The Old Cumberland Beggar*, *Mar-*

garet waiting in her ruined cottage for the husband who would never return, *Michael*, the old shepherd who stood, many and many a day, beside the unfinished sheepfold which he had begun to build with his lost boy,

"And never lifted up a single stone,"—

place these beside Millet's pictures, and the poems will bear the comparison.

Coleridge called Wordsworth "a miner of the human heart." But there is a striking peculiarity in his mining: he searched the most familiar places, by the most simple methods, to bring out the rarest and least suspected treasures. His discovery was that there is an element of poetry, like some metal of great value, diffused through the common clay of every-day life.

It is true that he did not always succeed in separating the precious metal from the surrounding dross. There were certain limitations in his mind which prevented him from distinguishing that which was familiar and precious, from that which was merely familiar.

One of these limitations was his lack of a sense

of humour. At a dinner-party he announced that he was never witty but once in his life. When asked to narrate the instance, after some hesitation he said: "Well, I will tell you. I was standing some time ago at the entrance of my cottage at Rydal Mount. A man accosted me with the question, 'Pray, sir, have you seen my wife pass by?' Whereupon I said, 'Why, my good friend, I didn't know till this moment that you had a wife!'" The humour of this story is unintentional and lies otherwhere than Wordsworth thought. The fact that he was capable of telling it as a merry jest accounts for the presence of many queer things in his poetry. For example; the lines in *Simon Lee*,

> "Few months of life has he in store
>   As he to you will tell,
> For still the more he works, the more
>   Do his weak ankles swell:"

the stanza in *Peter Bell*, which Shelley was accused of having maliciously invented, but which was actually printed in the first edition of the poem,

> "Is it a party in a parlour
> Cramming just as they on earth were crammed,
> Some sipping punch—some sipping tea

> But, as you by their faces see,
> All silent and all—damned?"

the couplet in the original version of *The Blind Highland Boy* which describes him as embarking on his voyage in

> "A household tub, like one of those
> Which women use to wash their clothes."

It is quite certain, I think, that Wordsworth's insensibility to the humourous side of things made him incapable of perceiving one considerable source of comfort and solace in lowly life. Plain and poor people get a great deal of consolation, in their hard journey, out of the rude but keen fun that they take by the way. The sense of humour is a means of grace.

I doubt whether Wordsworth's peasant-poetry has ever been widely popular among peasants themselves. There was an old farmer in the Lake Country who had often seen the poet and talked with him, and who remembered him well. Canon Rawnsley has made an interesting record of some of the old man's reminiscences. When he was asked whether he had ever read any of Wordsworth's poetry, or seen any of his books about in the farm-houses, he answered:

"Ay, ay, time or two. But ya're weel aware there's potry and potry. There's potry wi' a li'le bit pleasant in it, and potry sic as a man can laugh at or the childer understand, and some as takes a deal of mastery to make out what's said, and a deal of Wordsworth's was this sort, ye kna. You could tell fra the man's faace his potry would niver have no laugh in it."

But when we have admitted these limitations, it remains true that no other English poet has penetrated so deeply into the springs of poetry which rise by every cottage door, or sung so nobly of the treasures which are hidden in the humblest human heart, as Wordsworth has. This is his merit, his incomparable merit, that he has done so much, amid the hard conditions, the broken dreams, and the cruel necessities of life, to remind us how rich we are in being simply human.

Like Clifford, in the *Song at the Feast of Brougham Castle*,

"Love had he found in huts where poor men lie,"

and thenceforth his chosen task was to explore the
beauty and to show the power of that common love.

> "There is a comfort in the strength of love;
>   'Twill make a thing endurable, which else
>   Would overset the brain or break the heart."

He found the best portion of a good man's life in

> "His little, nameless, unremembered acts
>   Of kindness and of love."

In *The Old Cumberland Beggar* he declared

> "'Tis Nature's law
> That none, the meanest of created things,
> Of forms created the most vile and brute,
> The dullest or most noxious, should exist
> Divorced from good—a spirit and pulse of good,
> A life and soul, to every mode of being
> Inseparably linked."

And then he went on to trace, not always with full
poetic inspiration, but still with many touches of
beautiful insight, the good that the old beggar did
and received in the world, by wakening among the
peasants to whose doors he came from year to year,
the memory of past deeds of charity, by giving them
a sense of kinship with the world of want and sorrow, and by bestowing on them in their poverty

the opportunity of showing mercy to one whose needs were even greater than their own; for,—the poet adds—with one of those penetrating flashes which are the surest mark of his genius,—

"Man is dear to man; the poorest poor
Long for some moments in a weary life
When they can know and feel that they have been,
Themselves, the fathers and the dealers out
Of some small blessings; have been kind to such
As needed kindness, for this single cause
That we have all of us one human heart."

Nor did Wordsworth forget, in his estimate of the value of the simplest life, those pleasures which are shared by all men.

"Nuns fret not at their convent's narrow room;
And hermits are contented with their cells;
And students with their pensive citadels;
Maids at the wheel, the weaver at his loom,
Sit blithe and happy; bees that soar for bloom
High as the highest Peak of Furniss-fells,
Will murmur by the hour in fox-glove bells;
In truth the prison, unto which we doom
Ourselves, no prison is."

He sees a Miller dancing with two girls on the platform of a boat moored in the river Thames, and breaks out into a song on the "stray pleasures" that are spread through the earth to be claimed by whoever shall find them. A little crowd of poor people gather around a wandering musician in a city street, and the poet cries,

"Now, coaches and chariots! roar on like a stream;
  Here are twenty souls happy as souls in a dream;
  They are deaf to your murmurs—they care not for you,
  Nor what ye are flying, nor what ye pursue!"

He describes Coleridge and himself as lying together on the greensward in the orchard by the cottage at Grasmere, and says

  "If but a bird, to keep them company,
    Or butterfly sate down, they were, I ween,
    As pleased as if the same had been a maiden Queen."

It was of such simple and unchartered blessings that he loved to sing. He did not think that the vain or the worldly would care to listen to his voice. Indeed he said in a memorable passage of gentle scorn that he did not expect his poetry to be fashionable. "It is an awful truth," wrote he to Lady Beaumont, "that there neither is nor can be any genuine enjoyment of poetry among nineteen out of twenty of those persons who either live or wish to live in the broad light of the world,—among those who either are, or are striving to make themselves, people of consideration in society. This is a truth, and an awful one, because to be incapable of a feeling of poetry, in my sense of the word, is to be without love of human nature and reverence for God." He did not expect that his poetry would be popular in that world where men and women devote themselves to the business of pleasure, and where they care only for the things that minister to vanity or selfishness,—and it never was.

But there was another world where he expected to be welcome and of service. He wished his poetry to cheer the solitary, to uplift the downcast, to bid the despairing hope again, to teach the impoverished how much treasure was left to them. In short, he intended by the quiet ministry of his art to be one of those

"Poets who keep the world in heart,"

—and so he was.

It is impossible to exaggerate the value of such a service. Measured by any true and vital standard

Wordsworth's contribution to the welfare of mankind was greater, more enduring than that of the amazing Corsican, Bonaparte, who was born but a few months before him and blazed his way to glory. Wordsworth's service was to life at its fountain-head. His remedy for the despair and paralysis of the soul was not the prescription of a definite philosophy as an antidote. It was a hygienic method, a simple, healthful, loving life in fellowship with man and nature, by which the native tranquillity and vigour of the soul would be restored. The tendency of his poetry is to enhance our interest in humanity, to promote the cultivation of the small but useful virtues, to brighten our joy in common things, and to deepen our trust in a wise, kind, over-ruling God. Wordsworth gives us not so much a new scheme of life as a new sense of its interior and inalienable wealth. His calm, noble, lofty poetry is needed today to counteract the belittling and distracting influence of great cities; to save us from that most modern form of insanity, publicomania, which sacrifices all the sanctities of life to the craze for advertising; and to make a little quiet space in the heart, where those who are still capable of thought, in this age of clattering machinery, shall be able to hear themselves think.

V

But there is one still deeper element in Words-worth's poetry. He tells us very clearly that the true liberty and grandeur of *mankind* are to be found along the line of obedience to law and fidelity to duty. This is the truth which was revealed to him, slowly and serenely, as a consolation for the loss of his brief revolutionary dream. He learned to rejoice in it more and more deeply, and to proclaim it more and more clearly, as his manhood settled into firmness and strength.

Fixing his attention at first upon the humblest examples of the power of the human heart to resist unfriendly circumstances, as in *Resolution and Independence*, and to endure sufferings and trials, as in *Margaret* and *Michael*, he grew into a new conception of the right nobility. He saw that it was not necessary to make a great overturning of society before the individual man could begin to fulfil his destiny. "What then remains?" he cries—

> "To seek
> Those helps for his occasion ever near
> Who lacks not will to use them; vows, renewed
> On the first motion of a holy thought;
> Vigils of contemplation; praise; and prayer—
> A stream, which, from the fountain of the heart,
> Issuing however feebly, nowhere flows
> Without access of unexpected strength.
> But, above all, the victory is sure
> For him, who seeking faith by virtue, strives
> To yield entire submission to the law
> Of conscience—conscience reverenced and obeyed,
> As God's most intimate presence in the soul,
> And his most perfect image in the world."

If we would hear this message breathed in tones of lyric sweetness, as to the notes of a silver harp, we may turn to Wordsworth's poems on the Skylark,—

> "Type of the wise who soar, but never roam;
> True to the kindred points of Heaven and Home."

If we would hear it proclaimed with grandeur, as by a solemn organ; or with martial ardour, as by a ringing trumpet, we may read the *Ode to Duty* or *The Character of the Happy Warrior*, two of the noblest and most weighty poems that Wordsworth him, indeed that would need to be said if this were intended for a complete estimate of his influence. I should wish to speak of the deep effect which his poetry has had upon the style of other poets, breaking the bondage of "poetic diction" and leading the way to a simpler and more natural utterance. I should need to touch upon his alleged betrayal of his early revolutionary principles in politics, and to show, (if a paradox may be pardoned), that he never had them and that he always kept them. He never forsook liberty; he only changed his conception of it. He saw that the reconstruction of society must be preceded by reconstruction of the individual. Browning's stirring lyric, *The Lost Leader,*—

> "Just for a handful of silver he left us,
> Just for a ribbon to stick in his coat,"—

may have been written with Wordsworth in mind, but it was a singularly infelicitous suggestion of a remarkably good poem.

All of these additions would be necessary if this estimate were intended to be complete. But it is not, and so let it stand.

fulfil his destiny. "What then remains?" he cries—

> "To seek
> Those helps for his occasion ever near
> Who lacks not will to use them; vows, renewed
> On the first motion of a holy thought;
> Vigils of contemplation; praise; and prayer—
> A stream, which, from the fountain of the heart,
> Issuing however feebly, nowhere flows
> Without access of unexpected strength.
> But, above all, the victory is sure
> For him, who seeking faith by virtue, strives
> To yield entire submission to the law
> Of conscience—conscience reverenced and obeyed,
> As God's most intimate presence in the soul,
> And his most perfect image in the world."

If we would hear this message breathed in tones of lyric sweetness, as to the notes of a silver harp, we may turn to Wordsworth's poems on the Skylark,—

> "Type of the wise who soar, but never roam;
> True to the kindred points of Heaven and Home."

If we would hear it proclaimed with grandeur, as by a solemn organ; or with martial ardour, as by a ringing trumpet, we may read the *Ode to Duty* or *The Character of the Happy Warrior*, two of the noblest and most weighty poems that Wordsworth ever wrote. There is a certain distinction and elevation about his moral feelings which makes them in themselves poetic. In his poetry beauty is goodness and goodness is beauty.

But I think it is in the Sonnets that this element of Wordsworth's poetry finds the broadest and most perfect expression. For here he sweeps upward from the thought of the freedom and greatness of the individual man to the vision of nations and races emancipated and ennobled by loyalty to the right. How pregnant and powerful are his phrases! "Plain living and high thinking." "The homely beauty of the good old cause." "A few strong instincts and a few plain rules." "Man's unconquerable mind." "By the soul only, the Nations shall be great and free." The whole series of *Sonnets addressed to Liberty*, published in 1807, is full of poetic and prophetic fire. But none among them burns with a clearer light, none is more characteristic of him at his best, than that which is entitled *London, 1802.*

"Milton! thou should'st be living at this hour;
England hath need of thee; she is a fen

Of stagnant waters: altar, sword, and pen,
Fireside, the heroic wealth of hall and bower,
Have forfeited their ancient English dower
Of inward happiness. We are selfish men;
Oh! raise us up; return to us again;
And give us manners, virtue, freedom, power.
Thy soul was like a Star, and dwelt apart;
Thou had'st a voice whose sound was like the sea:
Pure as the naked heavens, majestic, free,
So didst thou travel on life's common way
In cheerful godliness; and yet thy heart
The lowliest duties on herself did lay."

This sonnet embraces within its "scanty plot of
ground" the roots of Wordsworth's strength. Here
is his view of nature in the kinship between the
lonely star and the solitary soul. Here is his recognition of life's common way as the path of honour,
and of the lowliest duties as the highest. Here is
his message that manners and virtue must go before freedom and power. And here is the deep spring
and motive of all his work, in the thought that *joy,
inward happiness*, is the dower that has been lost
and must be regained.

Here then I conclude this chapter on Wordsworth.
There are other things that might well be said about

him, indeed that would need to be said if this were intended for a complete estimate of his influence. I should wish to speak of the deep effect which his poetry has had upon the style of other poets, breaking the bondage of "poetic diction" and leading the way to a simpler and more natural utterance. I should need to touch upon his alleged betrayal of his early revolutionary principles in politics, and to show, (if a paradox may be pardoned), that he never had them and that he always kept them. He never forsook liberty; he only changed his conception of it. He saw that the reconstruction of society must be preceded by reconstruction of the individual. Browning's stirring lyric, *The Lost Leader*,—

> "Just for a handful of silver he left us,
>   Just for a ribbon to stick in his coat,"—

may have been written with Wordsworth in mind, but it was a singularly infelicitous suggestion of a remarkably good poem.

All of these additions would be necessary if this estimate were intended to be complete. But it is not, and so let it stand.

THE RECOVERY OF JOY

If we were to choose a motto for Wordsworth's poetry it might be this: "Rejoice, and again I say unto you, rejoice." And if we looked farther for a watchword, we might take it from that other great poet, Isaiah, standing between the fierce radicals and sullen conservatives of Israel, and saying,

"In quietness and confidence shall be your strength,
  In rest and in returning ye shall be saved."

"THE GLORY OF THE IMPERFECT"

"THE GLORY OF THE IMPERFECT"

ROBERT BROWNING'S POETRY

THERE is a striking contrast between the poetry of Browning and the poetry of Wordsworth; and this comes naturally from the difference between the two men in genius, temperament and life. I want to trace carefully and perhaps more clearly some of the lines of that difference. I do not propose to ask which of them ranks higher as poet. That seems to me a futile question. The contrast in kind interests me more than the comparison of degree. And this contrast, I think, can best be felt and understood through a closer knowledge of the central theme of each of the two poets.

Wordsworth is a poet of recovered joy. He brings consolation and refreshment to the heart,—consolation which is passive strength, refreshment which is peaceful energy. His poetry is addressed not to crowds, but to men standing alone, and feeling their loneliness most deeply when the crowd presses most tumultuously about them. He speaks to us one by one, distracted by the very excess of life, separated from humanity by the multitude of men, dazzled by the shifting variety of hues into which the eternal light is broken by the prism of the world,—one by one he accosts us, and leads us gently back, if we will follow him, into a more tranquil region and a serener air. There we find the repose of "a heart at leisure from itself." There we feel the unity of man and nature, and of both in God. There we catch sight of those eternal stars of truth whose shining, though sometimes hidden, is never dimmed by the cloud-confusions of mortality. Such is the mission of Wordsworth to the age. Matthew Arnold has described it with profound beauty.

> "He found us when the age had bound
> Our souls in its benumbing round,
> He spoke, and loosed our heart in tears.
> He laid us as we lay at birth
> On the cool flowery lap of earth,
> Smiles broke from us and we had ease,
> The hills were round us, and the breeze
> Went o'er the sun-lit fields again:
> Our foreheads felt the wind and rain.

Our youth returned; for there was shed
On spirits that had long been dead,
Spirits dried up and closely furled,
The freshness of the early world."

But precious as such a service is and ever must
be, it does not fill the whole need of man's heart.
There are times and moods in which it seems pale
and ineffectual. The very contrast between its
serenity, its assurance, its disembodied passion, its
radiant asceticism, and the mixed lights, the broken
music, the fluctuating faith, the confused conflict
of actual life, seems like a discouragement. It calls
us to go into a retreat, that we may find ourselves
and renew our power to live. But there are natures
which do not easily adapt themselves to a retreat,—
natures which crave stimulus more than consolation,
and look for a solution of life's problem that can be
worked out while they are in motion. They do not
wish, perhaps they are not able, to withdraw themselves from active life even for the sake of seeing
it more clearly.

Wordsworth's world seems to them too bare, too
still, too monotonous. The rugged and unpopulous

mountains, the lonely lakes, the secluded vales, do not attract them as much as the fertile plain with its luxuriant vegetation, the whirling city, the crowded highways of trade and pleasure. Simplicity is strange to them; complexity is their native element. They want music, but they want it to go with them in the march, the parade, the festal procession. The poet for them must be in the world, though he need not be altogether of it. He must speak of the rich and varied life of man as one who knows its artificial as well as its natural elements, —palaces as well as cottages, courts as well as sheepfolds. Art and politics and literature and science and churchmanship and society,—all must be familiar to him, material to his art, significant to his interpretation. His message must be modern and militant. He must not disregard doubt and rebellion and discord, but take them into his poetry and transform them. He must front

"The cloud of mortal destiny,"

and make the most of the light that breaks through it. Such a poet is Robert Browning; and his poetry

238

is the direct answer to at least one side of the modern *Zeitgeist*, restless, curious, self-conscious, energetic, the active, questioning spirit.

I

Browning's poetic work-time covered a period of about fifty-six years, (1833–1889,) and during this time he published over thirty volumes of verse, containing more than two hundred and thirty poems, the longest, *The Ring and the Book*, extending to nearly twenty-one thousand lines. It was an immense output, greater I think, in mass, than that of almost any other English poet except Shakespeare. The mere fact of such productiveness is worth noting, because it is a proof of the activity of the poet's mind, and also because it may throw some light upon certain peculiarities in the quality of his work.

Browning not only wrote much himself, he was also the cause of much writing in others. Commentaries, guide-books, handbooks, and expositions have grown up around his poetry so fast that the vines almost hide the trellis. The Browning Literature now demands not merely a shelf, but a whole case to itself in the library. It has come to such a pass that one must choose between reading the books that Browning wrote and the books that other people have written about Browning. Life is too short for both.

A reason, if not a justification, for this growth of a locksmith literature about his work is undoubtedly to be found in what Mr. Augustine Birrell calls "The Alleged Obscurity of Mr. Browning's Poetry." The adjective in this happy title indicates one of the points in the voluminous discussion. Does the difficulty in understanding Browning lie in him, or in his readers? Is it an accidental defect of his style, or a valuable element of his art, or an inherent profundity of his subject that makes him hard to read? Or does the trouble reside altogether in the imagination of certain readers, or perhaps in their lack of it? This question was debated so seriously as to become at times almost personal and threaten the unity of households if not the peace of nations. Browning himself was accustomed to tell the story of a young man who could not read his poetry, falling deeply in love with a young woman who would hardly read anything else. She made it a condition of her favour that her lover should learn to love her poet, and therefore set the marriage day at a point beyond the time when the bridegroom could present himself before her with convincing evidence that he had perused the works of Browning down to the last line. Such was the strength of love that the condition was triumphantly fulfilled. The poet used to tell with humourous satisfaction that he assisted in person at the wedding of these two lovers whose happiness he had unconsciously delayed and accomplished.

But an incident like this does not contribute much to the settlement of the controversy which it illustrates. Love is a notorious miracle-worker. The question of Browning's obscurity is still debatable; and whatever may be said on one side or the other, one fact must be recognized: it is not yet quite clear whether his poetry is clear or not.

To this fact I would trace the rise and flourishing of Browning Societies in considerable abundance, during the late Victorian Era, especially near Boston. The enterprise of reading and understanding

Browning presented itself as an affair too large and difficult for the intellectual capital of any private person. Corporations were formed, stock companies of intelligence were promoted, for the purpose of working the field of his poetry. The task which daunted the solitary individual was courageously undertaken by phalanxes and cheerfully pursued in fellowship. Thus the obscurity, alleged or actual, of the poet's writing, having been at first a hindrance, afterward became an advertisement to his fame. The charm of the enigma, the fascination of solving riddles, the pleasure of understanding something which other people at least professed to be unable to understand, entered distinctly into the growth of his popularity. A Browning cult, a Browning propaganda, came into being and toiled tremendously.

One result of the work of these clubs and societies is already evident: they have done much to remove the cause which called them into being. It is generally recognized that a considerable part of Browning's poetry is not really so difficult after all. It can be read and enjoyed by any one whose mind is in working order. Those innocent and stupid

Victorians were wrong about it. We alert and sagacious George-the-Fifthians need some tougher poetry to try our mettle. So I suppose the Browning Societies, having fulfilled their function, will gradually fade away,—or perhaps transfer their attention to some of those later writers who have put obscurity on a scientific basis and raised impenetrability to a fine art. Meantime I question whether all the claims which were made on behalf of Browning in the period of propaganda will be allowed at their face value. For example, that *The Ring and the Book* is "the greatest work of creative imagination that has appeared since the time of Shakespeare," * and that *A Grammarian's Funeral* is "the most powerful ode in English, the mightiest tribute ever paid to a man," † and that Browning's "style as it stands is God-made, not Browning-made," ‡ appear even now like drafts on glory which must be discounted before they are paid. Nor does it seem probable that the general proposition which

* Reverend A. H. Strong, *The Great Poets and their Theology*, p. 384.

† John Jay Chapman, *Emerson and Other Essays*, p. 195.

‡ J. H. Nettleship, *Robert Browning, Essays and Thoughts*, p. 292.

was sometimes advanced by extreme Browningites, (and others,) to the effect that all great poetry *ought* to be hard to read, and that a poem which is easy cannot be great, will stand the test of time. Milton's *Comus*, Gray's *Elegy*, Wordsworth's *Ode on the Intimations of Immortality*, Shelley's *Sky-lark*, Keats' *Grecian Urn*, and Tennyson's *Guinevere* cannot be reduced to the rank of minor verse by such a formula.

And yet it must be said that the very extravagance of the claims which were made for Browning, the audacity of enthusiasm which he inspired in his expositors, is a proof of the reality and the potency of his influence. Men are not kindled where there is no fire. Men do not keep on guessing riddles unless the answers have some interest and value. A stock company cannot create a prophet out of straw. Browning must have had something important to say to the age, and he must have succeeded in saying it in a way which was suitable, in spite of its defects, to convey his message, else we may be sure his age never would have listened to him, even by select companies, nor discussed him, even in a partisan temper, nor felt his influence, even at second-hand.

What was it, then, that he had to say, and how did he say it? What was the theme of his poetry, what the method by which he found it, what the manner in which he treated it, and what the central element of his disposition by which the development of his genius was impelled and guided? These are the questions,—questions of fact rather than of theory,—that particularly interest me in regard to Browning. And I hope it may be possible to consider them from a somewhat fresh point of view, and without entering into disturbing and unprofitable comparisons of rank with Shakespeare and the other poets.

But there is no reason why the answers to these questions should be concealed until the end of the chapter. It may be better to state them now, in order that we may be able to test them as we go on, and judge whether they are justified and how far they need to be qualified. There is a particular reason for taking this course, in the fact that Browning changed very little in the process of growth. There were alterations in his style, but there was no real alteration in the man, nor in his poetry. His first theme was his last theme. His early manner of treatment was his latest manner of treatment. What he said at the beginning he said again at the end. With the greatest possible variety of titles he had but one main topic; with the widest imaginable range of subjects, he used chiefly one method and reached but one conclusion; with a nature of almost unlimited breadth he was always under control of one central impulse and loyal to one central quality. Let me try, then, to condense the general impression into a paragraph and take up the particulars afterwards, point by point.

The clew to Browning's mind, it seems to me, is vivid and inexhaustible curiosity, dominated by a strangely steady optimism. His topic is not the soul, in the abstract, but souls in the concrete. His chosen method is that of spiritual drama, and for the most part, monodrama. His manner is the intense, subtle, passionate style of psychological realism. His message, uttered through the lips of

From a photograph, copyright by Hollyer, London.

ROBERT BROWNING.
Painted by G. F. Watts.

a hundred imaginary characters, but always with his own accent,—his message is "the Glory of the Imperfect."

II

The best criticisms of the poets have usually come from other poets, and often in the form of verse. Landor wrote of Browning,

> "Since Chaucer was alive and hale
> No man hath walked along our roads with step
> So active, so inquiring eye, or tongue
> So varied in discourse."

This is a thumb-nail sketch of Browning's personality,—not complete, but very lifelike. And when we add to it Landor's prose saying that "his is the surest foot since Chaucer's, that has waked the echoes from *the difficult places* of poetry and of life" we have a sufficiently plain clew to the unfolding of Browning's genius. Unwearying activity, intense curiosity, variety of expression, and a predominant interest in the difficult places of poetry and of life, —these were the striking characteristics of his mind. In his heart a native optimism, an unconquerable hopefulness, was the ruling factor. But of that I shall not speak until later, when we come to consider his message. For the present we are looking simply for the mainspring of his immense intellectual energy.

When I say that the clew to Browning's mind is to be found in his curiosity, I do not mean inquisitiveness, but a very much larger and nobler quality, for which we have no good word in English,—something which corresponds with the German *Wissbegier*, as distinguished from *Neugier:* an ardent desire to know things as they are, to penetrate as many as possible of the secrets of actual life. This, it seems to me, is the key to Browning's intellectual disposition. He puts it into words in his first poem *Pauline*, where he makes the nameless hero speak of his life as linked to

"a principle of restlessness
Which would be all, have, see, know, taste, feel, all—
This is myself; and I should thus have been
Though gifted lower than the meanest soul."

Paracelsus is only an expansion of this theme in the biography of a soul. In *Fra Lippo Lippi* the painter says:

"God made it all!
For what? Do you feel thankful, ay or no,
For this fair town's face, yonder river's line,
The mountain round it and the sky above,
Much more the figures of man, woman, child,
These are the frame to? What's it all about?
To be passed over, despised? Or dwelt upon,
Wondered at? oh, this last of course!—you say.
But why not do as well as say, paint these
Just as they are, careless what comes of it?
God's works—paint any one and count it crime
To let a truth slip.
      . . . This world's no blot for us,
Nor blank; it means intensely and means good:
To find its meaning is my meat and drink."

No poet was ever more interested in life than Browning, and whatever else may be said of his poetry it must be admitted that it is very interesting. He touches all sides of human activity and peers into the secret places of knowledge. He enters into the life of musicians in *Abt Vogler, Master Hugues of Saxe-Gotha, A Toccata of Galuppi's*, and *Charles Avison;* into the life of painters in *Andrea del Sarto, Pictor Ignotus, Fra Lippo Lippi, Old Pictures in Florence, Gerard de Lairesse, Pacchiarotto and How He Worked in Distemper*, and *Francis*

Furini; into the life of scholars in *A Grammarian's Funeral* and *Fust and his Friends;* into the life of politicians in *Prince Hohenstiel-Schwangau* and *George Bubb Dodington;* into the life of ecclesiastics in the *Soliloquy of the Spanish Cloister, Bishop Blougram's Apology, The Bishop orders his Tomb at Saint Praxed's Church,* and *The Ring and the Book;* and he makes excursions into all kinds of byways and crooked corners of life in such poems as *Mr. Sludge, the Medium, Porphyria's Lover, Mesmerism, Johannes Agricola in Meditation, Pietro of Abano, Ned Bratts, Jochanan Hakkadosh,* and so forth.

Merely to read a list of such titles is to have evidence of Browning's insatiable curiosity. It is evident also that he has a fondness for out-of-the-way places. He wants to know, even more than he wants to enjoy. If Wordsworth is the poet of the common life, Browning is the poet of the uncommon life. Extraordinary situations and eccentric characters attract him. Even when he is looking at some familiar scene, at some commonplace character, his effort is to discover something that shall prove that it is not familiar, not commonplace,—a singular detail, a striking feature, a mark of individuality. This gives him more pleasure than any distant vision of an abstraction or a general law.

"All that I know
    Of a certain star
Is, it can throw
    (Like the angled spar)
Now a dart of red,
    Now a dart of blue;
Till my friends have said
They would fain see, too,
    My star that dartles the red and the blue!
Then it stops like a bird; like a flower hangs furled;
    They must solace themselves with the Saturn above it.
What matter to me if their star is a world?
    Mine has opened its soul to me, therefore I love it."

One consequence of this penetrating, personal quality of mind is that Browning's pages teem with portraits of men and women, which are like sculptures and paintings of the Renaissance. They are more individual than they are typical. There is a peculiarity about each one of them which almost makes us forget to ask whether they have any general relation and value. The presentations are so sharp and vivid that their representative quality is lost.

If Wordsworth is the Millet of poetry, Browning is the Holbein or the Denner. He never misses the mole, the wrinkle, the twist of the eyebrow, which makes the face stand out alone, the sudden touch of self-revelation which individualizes the character. Thus we find in Browning's poetry few types of humanity, but plenty of men.

Yet he seldom, if ever, allows us to forget the background of society. His figures are far more individual than Wordsworth's, but far less solitary. Behind each of them we feel the world out of which they have come and to which they belong. There is a sense of crowded life surging through his poetry. The city, with all that it means, is not often completely out of view. "Shelley's characters," says a thoughtful essayist, "are creatures of wave and sky; Wordsworth's of green English fields; Browning's move in the house, the palace, the street." * In many of them, even when they are soliloquizing, there is a curious consciousness of opposition, of

* Miss Vida D. Scudder, *The Life of the Spirit in Modern English Poets.*

conflict. They seem to be defending themselves against unseen adversaries, justifying their course against the judgment of absent critics. Thus Bishop Blougram while he talks over the walnuts and the wine to Mr. Gigadibs, the sceptical hack-writer, has a worldful of religious conservatives and radicals in his eye and makes his half-cynical, wholly militant, apology for agnostic orthodoxy to them. The old huntsman, in *The Flight of the Duchess*, is maintaining the honour of his fugitive mistress against the dried-up, stiff, conventional society from which she has eloped with the Gypsies. Andrea del Sarto, looking at the soulless fatal beauty of his Lucrezia, and meditating on the splendid failure of his art, cries out to Rafael and Michelangelo and all his compeers to understand and judge him.

Even when Browning writes of romantic love, (one of his two favourite subjects), he almost always heightens its effect by putting it in relief against the ignorance, the indifference, the busyness, or the hostility of the great world. In *Cristina* and *Evelyn Hope* half the charm of the passion lies in the feeling that it means everything to the lover though no one else in the world may know of its existence. *Porphyria's Lover*, in a fit of madness, kills his mistress to keep her from going back to the world which would divide them. The sweet searching melody of *In a Gondola* plays itself athwart a sullen distant accompaniment of Venetian tyranny and ends with a swift stroke of vengeance from the secret Three.

Take, for an example of Browning's way of enhancing love by contrast, that most exquisite and subtle lyric called *Love Among the Ruins*.

"Where the quiet-coloured end of evening smiles
      Miles and miles
On the solitary pastures where our sheep
      Half asleep
Tinkle homeward through the twilight, stay or stop
      As they crop—
Was the site once of a city great and gay
      (So they say)
Of our country's very capital, its prince
      Ages since
Held his court in, gathered councils, wielding far
      Peace or war.

And I know, while thus the quiet-coloured eve
      Smiles to leave
To their folding, all our many-tinkling fleece
      In such peace,

And the slopes and rills in undistinguished gray
        Melt away—
That a girl with eager eyes and yellow hair
        Waits me there
In the turret whence the charioteers caught soul
        For the goal,
When the king looked, where she looks now, breathless,
    dumb
        Till I come.

.   .   .   .

In one year they sent a million fighters forth
        South and North,
And they built their gods a brazen pillar high
        As the sky,
Yet reserved a thousand chariots in full force—
        Gold of course.
Oh heart! Oh blood that freezes, blood that burns!
        Earth's returns
For whole centuries of folly, noise and sin!
        Shut them in,
With their triumphs and their glories and the rest!
        Love is best."

III

"Love is best!" That is one of the cardinal points of Browning's creed. He repeats it in a hundred ways: tragically in *A Blot in the 'Scutcheon;* sentimentally in *A Lover's Quarrel, Two in the Cam-*

pagna, The Last Ride Together; heroically in *Co-
lombe's Birthday;* in the form of a paradox in *The
Statue and the Bust;* as a personal experience in
By the Fireside, One Word More, and at the end of
the prelude to *The Ring and the Book.*

> "For life, with all it yields of joy and woe
>   And hope and fear, . . .
> Is just our chance o' the prize of learning love."

But it must be confessed that he does not often
say it as clearly, as quietly, as beautifully as in *Love
Among the Ruins.* For his chosen method is dramatic and his natural manner is psychological. So
ardently does he follow this method, so entirely
does he give himself up to this manner that his style

> "is subdued
> To what it works in, like the dyer's hand."

In the dedicatory note to *Sordello,* written in 1863,
he says "My stress lay in the incidents in the development of *a soul;* little else is worth study."
He felt intensely

> "How the world is made for each of us!
>   How all we perceive and know in it

> Tends to some moment's product thus,
>   When a soul declares itself—to wit,
>   By its fruit, the thing it does!"

In *One Word More* he describes his own poetry with keen insight:

> "Love, you saw me gather men and women,
>   Live or dead or fashioned by my fancy,
>   Enter each and all and use their service,
>   Speak from every mouth,—the speech a poem."

It is a mistake to say that Browning is a metaphysical poet: he is a psychological poet. His interest does not lie in the abstract problems of time and space, mind and matter, divinity and humanity. It lies in the concrete problems of opportunity and crisis, flesh and spirit, man the individual and God the person. He is an anatomist of souls.

> "Take the least man of all mankind, as I;
>   Look at his head and heart, find how and why
>   He differs from his fellows utterly." *

But his way of finding out this personal equation is not by observation and reflection. It is by throwing himself into the character and making it reveal

* Epilogue to *Dramatis Personæ*.

257

itself by intricate self-analysis or by impulsive action. What his poetry lacks is the temperate zone. He has the arctic circle of intellect and the tropics of passion. But he seldom enters the intermediate region of sentiment, reflection, sympathy, equable and prolonged feeling. Therefore it is that few of his poems have the power of "sinking inward from thought to thought" as Wordsworth's do. They surprise us, rouse us, stimulate us, more than they rest us. He does not penetrate with a mild and steady light through the portals of the human heart, making them transparent. He flings them wide open suddenly, and often the gates creak on their hinges. He is forever tying Gordian knots in the skein of human life and cutting them with the sword of swift action or intense passion. His psychological curiosity creates the difficulties, his intuitive optimism solves them.

IV

The results of this preoccupation with such subjects and of this manner of dealing with them may be recognized very easily in Browning's work.

First of all they turned him aside from becoming

a great Nature-poet, though he was well fitted to be one. It is not that he loves Nature's slow and solemn pageant less, but that he loves man's quick and varied drama more. His landscapes are like scenery for the stage. They accompany the unfolding of the plot and change with it, but they do not influence it. His observation is as keen, as accurate as Wordsworth's or Tennyson's, but it is less steady, less patient, less familiar. It is the observation of one who passes through the country but does not stay to grow intimate with it. The forms of nature do not print themselves on his mind; they flash vividly before him, and come and go. Usually it is some intense human feeling that makes the details of the landscape stand out so sharply. In *Pippa Passes*, it is in the ecstasy of love that Ottima and Sebald notice

> "The garden's silence: even the single bee
> Persisting in his toil, suddenly stopped,
> And where he hid you only could surmise
> By some campanula chalice set a-swing."

It is the sense of guilty passion that makes the lightning-flashes, burning through the pine-forest, seem like dagger-strokes,—

"As if God's messenger through the closed wood screen
Plunged and re-plunged his weapon at a venture,
Feeling for guilty thee and me."

In *Home Thoughts from Abroad*, it is the exile's deep
homesickness that brings the quick, delicate vision
before his eyes:

"Oh, to be in England
  Now that April's there,
  And whoever wakes in England
  Sees, some morning, unaware,
  That the lowest boughs and the brush-wood sheaf
  Round the elm-tree bole are in tiny leaf,
  While the chaffinch sings on the orchard bough
  In England—now!"

But Browning's touches of nature are not always
as happy as this. Often he crowds the details too
closely, and fails to blend them with the ground of
the picture, so that the tonality is destroyed and
the effect is distracting. The foreground is too
vivid: the aerial perspective vanishes. There is
an impressionism that obscures the reality. As
Amiel says: "Under pretense that we want to study
it more in detail, we pulverize the statue."

Browning is at his best as a Nature-poet in skyscapes, like the description of daybreak in *Pippa Passes*, the lunar rainbow in *Christmas Eve*, and the Northern Lights in *Easter Day;* and also in a kind of work which might be called symbolic landscape, where the imaginative vision of nature is made to represent a human experience. A striking example of this work is the scenery of *Childe Roland*, reflecting as in a glass the grotesque horrors of spiritual desolation. There is a passage in *Sordello* which makes a fertile landscape, sketched in a few swift lines, the symbol of Sordello's luxuriant nature; and another in Norbert's speech, in *In a Balcony*, which uses the calm self-abandonment of the world in the tranquil evening light as the type of the sincerity of the heart giving itself up to love. But perhaps as good an illustration as we can find of Browning's quality as a Nature-poet, is a little bit of mystery called *Meeting at Night*.

> "The gray sea and the long black land;
>   And the yellow half-moon, large and low;
>   And the startled little waves that leap
>   In fiery ringlets from their sleep,
>   As I gain the cove with pushing prow,
>   And quench its speed in the slushy sand.

Then a mile of warm sea-scented beach;
Three fields to cross till a farm appears;
A tap at the pane, the quick sharp scratch
And the blue spirt of a lighted match,
And a voice less loud, through its joys and fears,
Than the two hearts beating each to each!"

This is the landscape of the drama.

A second result of Browning's preoccupation with dramatic psychology is the close concentration and "alleged obscurity" of his style. Here again I evade the critical question whether the obscurity is real, or whether it is only a natural and admirable profundity to which an indolent reviewer has given a bad name. That is a question which Posterity must answer. But for us the fact remains that some of his poetry is hard to read; it demands close attention and strenuous effort; and when we find a piece of it that goes very easily, like *The Pied Piper of Hamelin*, *How They brought the Good News from Ghent to Aix*, *Hervé Riel*, or the stirring *Cavalier Tunes*, we are conscious of missing the sense of strain which we have learned to associate with the reading of Browning.

One reason for this is the predominance of

curiosity over harmony in his disposition. He tries to express the inexpressible, to write the unwritable. As Dr. Johnson said of Cowley, he has the habit "of pursuing his thoughts to the last ramifications, by which he loses the grandeur of generality." Another reason is the fluency, the fertility, the haste of his genius, and his reluctance, or inability, to put the brakes on his own productiveness.

It seems probable that if Browning had been able to write more slowly and carefully he might have written with more lucidity. There was a time when he made a point of turning off a poem a day. It is doubtful whether the story of *The Ring and the Book* gains in clearness by being told by eleven different persons, all of them inclined to volubility.

Yet Browning's poetry is not verbose. It is singularly condensed in the matter of language. He seems to have made his most arduous effort in this direction. After *Paracelsus* had been published and pronounced "unintelligible," he was inclined to think that there might be some fault of too great terseness in the style. But a letter from Miss Caroline Fox was shown to him, in which that lady, (then very young,) took the opposite view and asked "doth he know that Wordsworth will devote a fortnight or more to the discovery of the single word that is the one fit for his sonnet." Browning appears to have been impressed by this criticism; but he set himself to work upon it, not so much by way of selecting words as by way of compressing them. He put *Sordello* into a world where many of the parts of speech are lacking and all are crowded. He learned to pack the largest possible amount of meaning into the smallest possible space, as a hasty traveller packs his portmanteau. Many small articles are crushed and crumpled out of shape. He adopted a system of elisions for the sake of brevity, and loved, as C. S. Calverley said,

> "to dock the smaller parts of speech
> As we curtail th' already curtailed cur."

At the same time he seldom could resist the temptation to put in another thought, another simile, another illustration, although the poem might be already quite full. He called out, like the conductor of a street-car, "Move up in front: room for one more!" He had little tautology of expression, but much of conception. A good critic says "Browning condenses by the phrase, elaborates by the volume." *

One consequence of this system of writing is that a great deal of Browning's poetry lends itself admirably to translation,—into English. The number of prose paraphrases of his poems is great, and so constantly increasing that it seems as if there must be a real demand for them. But Coleridge, speaking of the qualities of a true poetic style, remarked: "Whatever lines can be translated into other words of the same language without diminution of their significance, either in sense, or in association, or in any other feeling, are so far vicious in their diction."

Another very notable thing in Browning's poetry is his fertility and fluency of rhyme. He is probably the most rapid, ingenious, and unwearying rhymer among the English poets. There is a story that once, in company with Tennyson, he was challenged to produce a rhyme for "rhinoceros," and almost instantly accomplished the task with a verse in

* Cheney, *The Golden Guess*, p. 143.

which the unwieldy quadruped kept time and tune with the phrase "he can toss Eros." * There are other *tours de force* almost as extraordinary in his serious poems. Who but Browning would have thought of rhyming "syntax" with "tin-tacks," or "spare-rib" with "Carib," (*Flight of Duchess*) or "Fra Angelico's" with "bellicose," or "Ghirlandajo" with "heigh-ho," (*Old Pictures in Florence*) or "expansive explosive" with "O Danaides, O Sieve!" (*Master Hugues*). Rhyme, with most poets, acts as a restraint, a brake upon speech. But with Browning it is the other way. His rhymes are like wild, froliesome horses, leaping over the fences and carrying him into the widest digressions. Many a couplet, many a stanza would not have been written but for the impulse of a daring, suggestive rhyme.

Join to this love of somewhat reckless rhyming, his deep and powerful sense of humour, and you have the secret of his fondness for the grotesque. His poetry abounds in strange contrasts, sudden changes of mood, incongruous comparisons, and odd presentations of well-known subjects. Some-

* *Memoir of Alfred Lord Tennyson*, vol. II, p. 230.

times the whole poem is written in this manner.
The *Soliloquy in a Spanish Cloister, Sibrandus Schaf-
naburgensis*, and *Caliban upon Setebos*, are poetic
gargoyles. Sometimes he begins seriously enough,
as in the poem on Keats, and closes with a bit of
fantastic irony:

> "Hobbs hints blue,—straight he turtle eats:
>   Nobbs prints blue,—claret crowns his cup:
> Nokes outdares Stokes in azure feats—
>   Both gorge. Who fished the murex up?
> What porridge had John Keats?"

Sometimes the poem opens grotesquely, like *Christmas Eve*, and rises swiftly to a wonderful height of
pure beauty and solemnity, dropping back into a
grotesque at the end. But all this play of fancy
must not be confused with the spirit of mockery or
of levity. It is often characteristic of the most serious and earnest natures; it arises in fact from the
restlessness of mind in the contemplation of evil,
or from the perception of life's difficulties and perplexities. Shakespeare was profoundly right in introducing the element of the grotesque into *Hamlet*,
his most thoughtful tragedy. Browning is never

really anything else but a serious thinker, passionately curious to solve the riddle of existence. Like his own *Sordello* he

> "Gave to familiar things a face grotesque,
>   Only, pursuing through the mad burlesque,
>   A grave regard."

We may sum up, then, what we have to say of Browning's method and manner by recognizing that they belong together and have a mutual fitness and inevitableness. We may wish that he had attained to more lucidity and harmony of expression, but we should probably have had some difficulty in telling him precisely how to do it, and he would have been likely to reply with good humour as he did to Tennyson, "The people must take me as they find me." If he had been less ardent in looking for subjects for his poetry, he might have given more care to the form of his poems. If he had cut fewer blocks, he might have finished more statues. The immortality of much of his work may be discounted by its want of perfect art,—the only true preservative of man's handiwork. But the immortality of his genius is secure. He may not be ranked

"GLORY OF THE IMPERFECT"

finally among the great masters of the art of poetry. But he certainly will endure as a mine for poets. They may stamp the coins more clearly and fashion the ornaments more delicately. But the gold is his. He was the prospector,—the first dramatic psychologist of modern life. The very imperfections of his work, in all its splendid richness and bewildering complexity, bear witness to his favourite doctrine that life itself is more interesting than art, and more glorious, because it is not yet perfect.

V

"The Glory of the Imperfect,"—that is a phrase which I read in a pamphlet by that fine old Grecian and noble Christian philosopher, George Herbert Palmer, many years ago. It seems to me to express the central meaning of Browning's poetry.

He is the poet of aspiration and endeavour; the prophet of a divine discontent. All things are precious to him, not in themselves, but as their defects are realized, as man uses them, and presses through them, towards something higher and better. Hope is man's power: and the things hoped for must be as yet unseen. Struggle is man's life; and the purpose of life is not merely education, but a kind of progressive creation of the soul.

"Man partly is and wholly hopes to be."

The world presents itself to him, as the Germans say, *Im Werden*. It is a world of potencies, working itself out. Existence is not the mere fact of being, but the vital process of becoming. The glory of man lies in his power to realize this process in his mind and to fling himself into it with all his will. If he tries to satisfy himself with things as they are, like the world-wedded soul in *Easter Eve*, he fails. If he tries to crowd the infinite into the finite, like Paracelsus, he fails. He must make his dissatisfaction his strength. He must accept the limitations of his life, not in the sense of submitting to them, but as Jacob wrestled with the angel, in order to win, through conflict, a new power, a larger blessing. His ardent desires and longings and aspirations, yes, even his defeats and disappointments and failures, are the stuff out of which his immortal destiny is weaving itself. The one thing that life requires of him is to act with ardour, to go forward resolutely, to "burn his way through the world"; and the great lesson which it teaches him is this:

> "But thou shalt painfully attain to joy
> While hope and love and fear shall keep thee man."

Browning was very much needed in the Nineteenth Century as the antidote, or perhaps it would be more just to say, as the complement to Carlyle. For Carlyle's prophecy, with all its moral earnestness, its virility, its indomitable courage, had in it a ground-tone of despair. It was the battle-cry of a forlorn hope. Man must hate shams intensely, must seek reality passionately, must do his duty desperately; but he can never tell why. The reason of things is inscrutable: the eternal Power that rules things is unknowable. Carlyle, said Mazzini, "has a constant disposition to crush the human by comparing him with God." But Browning has an unconquerable disposition to elevate the human by joining him to God. The power that animates and governs the world is Divine; man cannot escape from it nor overcome it. But the love that stirs in man's heart is also Divine; and if man will follow it, it shall lead him to that height where he shall see that Power is Love.

> "I have faith such end shall be:
>   From the first Power was—I knew.
> Life has made clear to me
>   That, strive but for closer view,
> Love were as plain to see.
>
> When see? When there dawns a day
>   If not on the homely earth,
> Then yonder, worlds away,
>   Where the strange and new have birth
> And Power comes full in play." *

Browning's optimism is fundamental. Originally a matter of temperament, perhaps, as it is expressed in *At the Mermaid*,—

> "I find earth not gray, but rosy,
>   Heaven not grim but fair of hue.
> Do I stoop? I pluck a posy,
>   Do I stand and stare? All's blue——"

primarily the spontaneous tone of a healthy, happy nature, it became the chosen key-note of all his music, and he works it out through a hundred harmonies and discords. He is "sure of goodness as of life." He does not ask "How came good into

* *Asolando*, "Reverie."

272

the world?" For that, after all, is the pessimistic question; it assumes that the ground of things is evil and the good is the breaking of the rule. He asks instead "How came evil into the world?" That is the optimistic question; as long as a man puts it in that form he is an optimist at heart; he takes it for granted that good is the native element and evil is the intruder; there must be a solution of the problem whether he can find it or not; the rule must be superior to, and triumphant over, the exception; the meaning and purpose of evil must somehow, some time, be proved subordinate to good.

That is Browning's position:

> "My own hope is, a sun will pierce
> The thickest cloud earth ever stretched;
> That, after Last, returns the First,
> Though a wide compass round be fetched;
> That what began best, can't end worst,
> Nor what God blessed once prove accurst."

The way in which he justifies this position is characteristic of the man. His optimism is far less defensive than it is militant. He never wavers from his intuitive conviction that "the world means good." He follows this instinct as a soldier follows his banner, into whatever difficulties and conflicts it may lead him, and fights his way out, now with the weapons of philosophy, now with the bare sword of faith.

VI

It might seem at first as if it were unfair to attempt any estimate of the philosophic and religious teaching of a poet like Browning, whose method we have already recognized as dramatic. Can we ascribe to the poet himself the opinions which he puts into the mouths of his characters? Can we hold him responsible for the sentiments which are expressed by the actors on his stage?

Certainly this objection must be admitted as a restraint in the interpretation of his poetry. We are not to take all that his characters say, literally and directly, as his own belief, any more than we are to read the speeches of Satan, and Eliphaz, and Bildad, and Zophar, in the Book of Job, as utterances of the spirit of inspiration. But just as that great dramatic Scripture, dealing with the problems of evil and suffering and sovereignty, does contain a doctrine and convey a lesson, so the poetry of Browning, taken as a whole, utters a distinct and positive prophetic message.

In the first place, many of the poems are evidently subjective, written without disguise in the first person. Among these we may consider *My Star; By the Fireside; One Word More;* the Epilogues to *Dramatis Personæ* and *Pachiarrotto* and *Ferishtah's Fancies;* the introduction and the close of *The Ring and the Book; Christmas Eve* and *Easter Day;* the ending of the poem called *Gold Hair,* and of *A Death in the Desert,* and of *Bishop Blougram's Apology; Prospice* and *Reverie.* In the second place we must remember Goethe's dictum: "Every author in some degree, pourtrays himself in his works, even be it against his will." Even when Browning is writing dramatically, he cannot conceal his sympathy. The masks are thin. His eyes shine through. "His own personality," says Mr. Stedman, "is manifest in the speech and movement of almost every character of each piece. His spirit is infused as if by metempsychosis, within them all, and forces each to assume a strange Pentecostal tone, which we discover to be that of the poet himself." Thus it is not impossible, nor even difficult, to reach a fair estimate of his ethical and religious teaching and discover its principal elements.

1. First among these I would put a great confidence in God. Browning is the most theological of modern poets. The epithet which was applied to Spinoza might well be transferred to him. He is a "God-intoxicated" man. But in a very different sense, for whereas the philosopher felt God as an idea, the poet feels Him intensely as a person. The song which he puts into the lips of the unconscious heroine in *Pippa Passes*,—

> "God's in his heaven
> All's right with the world,——"

is the recurrent theme of his poetry. He cries with Paracelsus,

"God thou art Love, I build my faith on that."

Even when his music is broken and interrupted by discords, when it seems to dissolve and fade away as all human work, in its outward form, dissolves

and fades, he turns, as Abt Vogler turns from his
silent organ, to God;

> "Therefore to whom turn I but to thee, the ineffable
>   Name?
>   Builder and maker, thou, of houses not made with
>   hands!
> What, have fear of change from thee who art ever the
>   same?
>   Doubt that thy power can fill the heart that thy
>   power expands?"

In *Rabbi Ben Ezra* he takes up the ancient figure
of the potter and the clay and uses it to express
his boundless trust in God.

The characteristic mark of Browning's view of
God is that it is always taken from the side of humanity. The Perfect Glory is the correlative of
the glory of the imperfect. The Divine Love is
the answer to the human longing. God is, because
man needs Him. From this point of view it almost
seems, as a brilliant essayist has said, as if "In
Browning, God is adjective to man." *

But it may be said in answer, that, at least for
man, this is the only point of view that is accessible.

* J. J. Chapman, *Emerson, and Other Essays.*

We can never leave our own needs behind us, however high we may try to climb. Certainly if we succeed in forgetting them for a moment, in that very moment we have passed out of the region of poetry, which is the impassioned interpretation of man's heart.

2. The second element of power in Browning's poetry is that he sees in the personal Christ the very revelation of God that man's heart most needs and welcomes. Nowhere else in all the range of modern poetry has this vision been expressed with such spiritual ardour, with such poignant joy. We must turn back to the pages of Isaiah to find anything to equal the Messianic rapture of the minstrel in *Saul*.

"He who did most shall bear most: the strongest shall
    stand the most weak.
'Tis the weakness in strength that I cry for! my flesh
    that I seek
In the Godhead! I seek and I find it. O Saul, it shall
    be,
A Face like my face that receives thee; a man like to
    me,
Thou shalt love and be loved by, forever: a Hand like
    this hand

Shall throw open the gates of new life to thee! see the
    Christ stand!"

We must look into the Christ-filled letters of St.
Paul to find the attractions of the Crucified One
uttered as powerfully as they are in the *Epistle of
Karshish*.

"The very God! think Abib; dost thou think?
So, the All-great, were the All-Loving too—
So, through the thunder comes a human voice
Saying, ' O heart I made, a heart beats here!
Face, my hands fashioned, see it in myself!
Thou hast no power, nor mayest conceive of mine,
But love I gave thee, with myself to love,
And thou must love me who have died for thee!' "

It is idle to assert that these are only dramatic
presentations of the Christian faith. No poet could
have imagined such utterances without feeling their
significance; and the piercing splendour of their
expression discloses his sympathy. He reveals it
yet more unmistakably in *Christmas Eve*, (strophe
XVII) and in *Easter Day*, (strophe XXX.) In the
Epilogue to *Dramatis Personæ* it flashes out clearly.
The second speaker, as Renan, has bewailed the
vanishing of the face of Christ from the sorrowful

vision of the race. The third speaker, the poet himself, answers:

> "That one Face, far from vanish, rather grows,
>   Or decomposes but to recompose
>   Become my universe that feels and knows!"

"That face," said Browning to a friend, "that face is the face of Christ: that is how I feel Him."

Surely this is the religious message that the world most needs to-day. More and more everything in Christianity hangs upon the truth of the Incarnation. The alternative declares itself. Either no God whom we can know and love at all, or God personally manifest in Christ!

3. The third religious element in Browning's poetry is his faith that this life is a probation, a discipline for the future. He says, again and again,

> "I count life just a stuff
> To try the soul's strength on, educe the man."

The glory of the imperfect lies in the power of progress, "man's distinctive mark." And progress comes by conflict; conflict with falsehood and ignorance,—

> "Living here means nescience simply; 'tis next life that
>   helps to learn——"

and conflict with evil,—

"GLORY OF THE IMPERFECT"

"Why comes temptation but for man to meet,
   And master and make crouch beneath his foot,
   And so be pedestalled in triumph?"

The poet is always calling us to be glad we are engaged in such a noble strife.

"Rejoice we are allied
   To that which doth provide
And not partake, effect and not receive!
   A spark disturbs our clod;
   Nearer we hold of God
Who gives, than of his tribes that take, I must believe.

Then welcome each rebuff
   That turns earth's smoothness rough,
Each sting that bids nor sit nor stand but go!
   Be our joys three-parts pain!
   Strive and hold cheap the strain;
Learn, nor account the pang; dare, never grudge the
   throe!"

Now this is fine doctrine, lofty, strenuous, stimulating. It appeals to the will, which is man's central power. It proclaims the truth that virtue must be active in its essence though it may also be passive in its education, positive in its spirit and negative only by contrast.

But it is in the working out of this doctrine into

an ethical system that Browning enters upon dangerous ground, and arrives at results which seem to obscure the clearness, and to threaten the stability of the moral order, by which alone, if the world's greatest teachers have been right, the ultimate good of humanity can be attained. Here, it seems to me, his teaching, especially in its latter utterances, is often confused, turbulent, misleading. His light is mixed with darkness. He seems almost to say that it matters little which way we go, provided only we go.

He overlooks the deep truth that there is an activity of the soul in self-restraint as well as in self-assertion. It takes as much courage to dare not to do evil as it does to dare to do good. The hero is sometimes the man who stands still. Virtue is noblest when it is joined to virility. But virility alone is not virtue nor does it always lead to moral victory. Sometimes it leads straight towards moral paralysis, death, extinction. Browning fails to see this, because his method is dramatic and because he dramatizes through himself. He puts himself into this or the other character, and works himself out through it, preserving still in himself, though all unconsciously, the soul of something good. Thus he does not touch that peculiar deadening of spiritual power which is one result of the unrestrained following of impulse and passion. It is this defect in his vision of life that leads to the dubious and interrogatory moral of such a poem as *The Statue and the Bust*.

Browning values the individual so much that he lays all his emphasis upon the development of stronger passions and aspirations, the unfolding of a more vivid and intense personality, and has comparatively little stress to lay upon the larger thought of the progress of mankind in harmony and order. Indeed he poetizes so vigorously against the conventional judgments of society that he often seems to set himself against the moral sentiments on which those conventional judgments, however warped, ultimately rest. "Over and over again in Browning's poetry," says a penetrating critic, "we meet with this insistence on the value of moments of high excitement, of intense living, of full experience of pleasure, even though such moments be of the essence of evil and fruitful in all dark consequences."

Take for example his treatment of love. He is right in saying "Love is best." But is he right in admitting, even by inference, that love has a right to take its own way of realizing itself? Can love be at its best unless it is obedient to law? Does it not make its truest music when it keeps its place in the harmony of purity and peace and good living? Surely the wild and reckless view of love as its own law which seems to glimmer through the unconsumed smoke of Browning's later poems, such as *Fifine at the Fair*, *The Inn Album*, and *Red Cotton Nightcap Country*, needs correction by a true flash of insight like that which we find in two lines of *One Word More*:

> *"Dante, who loved well because he hated,*
> *Hated wickedness that hinders loving."*

Browning was at times misled by a perilous philosophy into a position where the vital distinction between good and evil dissolved away in a cloud of unreality. In *Ferishtah's Fancies* and *Parleyings with Certain People of Importance*, any one who has the patience to read them will find himself in a nebulous moral world. The supposed necessity of showing that evil is always a means to good tempts to the assertion that it has no other reality. Perhaps it is altogether an illusion, needed to sting us into conflict, but really non-existent. Perhaps it is only the shadow cast by the good,—or "the silence implying sound." Perhaps it is good in disguise, not yet developed from the crawling worm into the creature with wings. After this fashion the whimsical dervish Ferishtah strews his beans upon the table.

> "This bean was white, this—black,
> Set by itself,—but see if good and bad
> Each following other in companionship,
> Black have not grown less black and white less white,
> Till blackish seems but dun, and whitish,—gray,
> And the whole line turns—well, or black to thee
> Or white alike to me—no matter which."

Certainly if this were the essence of Browning's poetry the best safeguard against its falsehood would be its own weakness. Such a message, if this were all, could never attract many hearers, nor inspire those whom it attracted. Effort, struggle, noble conflict would be impossible in a world where there were no moral certainties or realities, but all men felt that they were playing at a stupid game like the Caucus race in *Alice in Wonderland*, where everything went round in a circle and every runner received a prize.

But in fact these elements of weakness in Browning's work, as it seems to me, do not belong to his true poetry. They are expressed, generally, in his most obfuscated style, and at a prohibitory length. They are embodied in poems which no one is likely to read for fun, and few are capable of learning by heart.

But when we go back to his best work we find another spirit, we hear another message. Clear, resonant, trumpet-like his voice calls to us proclaiming the glorious possibilities of this imperfect life. Only do not despair; only do not sink down into conventionality, indifference, mockery, cynicism; only rise and hope and go forward out of the house of bondage into the land of liberty. True, the prophecy is not complete. But it is inspiring. He does not teach us how to live. But he does tell us to live,—with courage, with love to man, with trust in God,—and he bids us find life glorious, because it is still imperfect and therefore full of promise.

A QUAINT COMRADE BY QUIET STREAMS

A QUAINT COMRADE BY QUIET STREAMS

IN April, 1653, Oliver Cromwell, after much bloodshed and amid great confusion, violently dissolved the "Rump Parliament." In May of the same year, Izaak Walton published *The Compleat Angler, or the Contemplative Man's Recreation.* 'Twas a strange contrast between the tranquil book and the tempestuous time. But that the contrast was not displeasing may be inferred from the fact that five editions were issued during the author's life, which ended in 1683, at the house of his son-in-law in the cathedral close at Winchester, Walton being then in his ninety-first year and at peace with God and man.

Doubtless one of the reasons why those early editions, especially the first, the second, and the fifth, (in which Walton's friend Charles Cotton added his "Instructions How to Angle for a Trout or Grayling in a Clear Stream,") are now become so rare and costly, is because they were carried about by honest anglers of the 17th Century in their coat-pockets or in their wallets, a practice whereby the body of a book is soon worn out, though its soul be immortal.

That this last is true of Walton's *Angler* seems proven by its continual reappearance. The Hundredth Edition (called after the rivers Lea and Dove, which Walton loved) was brought out in 1888, by the genial fisherman and bibliophile, R. B. Marston of the London *Fishing Gazette*. Among the other English editions I like John Major's second (1824); and Sir John Hawkins', reissued by Bagster (1808); and Pickering's richly illustrated two volumes edited by Sir Harris Nicolas (1836). There is a 32mo reprint by the same publisher, (and a "diamond" from the Oxford University Press,) small enough to go comfortably in a vest-pocket with your watch or your pipe. I must speak also of the admirable introductions to the *Angler* written in these latter years by James Russell Lowell, Andrew Lang, and Richard Le Gallienne; and of the great American edition made by the Reverend Doctor

A QUAINT COMRADE

George W. Bethune in 1847, a work in which the learning, wit, and sympathy of the editor illuminate the pages. This edition is already hard to find, but no collector of angling books would willingly go without it.

The gentle reader has a wide choice, then, of the form in which he will take his Walton,—something rare and richly adorned for the library, or something small and plain for the pocket or the creel. But in what shape soever he may choose to read the book, if he be not "a severe, sour-complexioned man" he will find it good company. There is a most propitiating paragraph in the "Address" at the beginning of the first edition. Explaining why he has introduced "some innocent harmless mirth" into his work, Walton writes:

"I am the willinger to justify this innocent mirth because the whole discourse is a kind of picture of my own disposition, at least of my disposition in such days and times as I allow myself, when honest *Nat.* and *R.R.* and I go a-fishing together."

This indeed is one of the great attractions of the book, that it so naturally and simply shows the author. I know of no other in which this quality of self-revelation without pretense or apology is as modest and engaging,—unless it be the *Essays* of Charles Lamb, or those of M. de Montaigne. We feel well acquainted with Walton when we have read the *Angler*, and perhaps have added to our reading his only other volume,—a series of brief *Lives* of certain excellent and beloved men of his time, wherein he not only portrays their characters but further discloses his own. They were men of note in their day: Sir Henry Wotton, ambassador to Venice; Dr. John Donne, Dean of St. Paul's; Richard Hooker, famous theologian; George Herbert, sacred poet; Bishop Sanderson, eminent churchman. With most of these, and with other men of like standing, Walton was in friendship. The company he kept indicates his quality. Whatever his occupation or his means, he was certainly a gentleman and a scholar, as well as a good judge of fishing.

Of the actual events of his life, despite diligent research, little is known, and all to his credit. Perhaps there were no events of public importance or interest. He came as near as possible to the fortu-

nate estate of the nation which has a good repute
but no history.

He was born in the town of Stafford, August 9th,
1593. Of his schooling he speaks with becoming
modesty; and it must have been brief, for at the
age of sixteen or seventeen he was an apprentice in
London. Whether he was a linendraper or an iron-
monger is a matter of dispute. Perhaps he was first
one and then the other. His first shop, in the Royal
Burse, Cornhill, was about seven and a half feet
long by five wide. But he must have done a good
business in those narrow quarters; for in 1624 he
had a better place on Fleet Street, and from 1628 to
1644 he was a resident of the parish of St. Dunstan's, having a comfortable dwelling (and probably
his shop) in Chancery Lane, "about the seventh
house on the left hand side." He served twice on
the grand jury, and was elected a vestryman of St.
Dunstan's twice.

It was during his residence here that he lost his
first wife, Rachel Floud, and the seven children
whom she had borne to him. In 1644, finding the
city "dangerous for honest men" on account of the

civil strife and disorder, he retired from London, and probably from business, and lived in the country, "sometimes at Stafford," (according to Anthony Wood, the antiquary,) "but mostly in the families of the eminent clergymen of England, of whom he was much beloved." This life gave him large opportunity for his favourite avocation of fishing, and widened the circle of his friendships, for wherever he came as a guest he was cherished as a friend. I make no doubt that the love of angling, to which innocent recreation he was attached by a temperate and enduring passion, was either the occasion or the promoter of many of these intimacies. For it has often been observed that this sport inclines those that practise it to friendliness; and there are no closer or more lasting companionships than such as are formed beside flowing streams by men who study to be quiet and go a-fishing.

After his second marriage, about 1646, to Anne Ken, half-sister of Bishop Thomas Ken, (author of the well-known hymns, "Awake, my soul, and with the sun," and "All praise to Thee, my God, this night,") Walton went to live for some years at

Clerkenwell. While he was there, the book for which he had been long preparing, *The Compleat Angler*, was published, and gave him his sure place in English literature and in the heart of an innumerable company of readers.

Never was there a better illustration of "fisherman's luck" than the success of Walton's book. He set out to make a little "discourse of fish and fishing," a "pleasant curiositie" he calls it, full of useful information concerning the history and practice of the gentle art, and, as the author modestly claims on his title-page, "not unworthy the perusal of most anglers." Instead of this he produced an imperishable classic, which has been read with delight by thousands who have never wet a line. It was as if a man went forth to angle for smelts and caught a lordly salmon.

As a manual of practical instruction the book is long since out of date. The kind of rod which Walton describes is too cumbrous for the modern angler, who catches his trout with a split bamboo weighing no more than four or five ounces, and a thin waterproofed line of silk beside which Father Izaak's favourite line twisted of seven horse-hairs would look like a bed-cord. Most of his recipes for captivating baits and lures, and his hints about "oyl," or "camphire" with which they may be made infallibly attractive to reluctant fish, are now more curious than valuable. They seem like ancient superstitions,—although this very summer I have had recommended to me a secret magic ointment one drop of which upon a salmon-fly would (supposedly) render it irresistible. (Yes, reader, I did try it; but its actual effect, owing to various incalculable circumstances, could not be verified. The salmon took the anointed fly sometimes, but at other times they took the unanointed, and so I could not make affidavit that it was the oil that allured them. It may have been some tickling in the brain, some dim memory of the time when they were little parr, living in fresh water for their first eighteen months and feeding mainly on floating insects, that made them wish to rise again.)

But to return to my subject. The angler of to-day who wishes to understand the technics of modern fishing-gear will go to such books as H. B. Wells'

Fly Rods and Fly Tackle, or to Dr. George Holden's
The Idyl of the Split Bamboo. This very year two
volumes have been published, each of which in its
way goes far beyond Walton: Mr. William Rad-
cliffe's *Fishing from the Earliest Times*, which will
undoubtedly take its place as the standard history
of the ancient craft of fish-catching; and Mr. Edward
R. Hewitt's *Secrets of the Salmon*, a brilliant and
suggestive piece of work, full of acute scientific observation and successful experiment. These belong
to what De Quincey called "the literature of knowledge." But the *Angler* belongs to "the literature of
power,"—that which has a quickening and inspiring
influence upon the spirit,—and here it is unsurpassed,
I may even say unrivalled, by any book ever written
about any sport. Charles Lamb wrote to Coleridge
commending it to his perusal: "It might sweeten a
man's temper at any time to read *The Compleat
Angler*."

The unfailing charm of the book lives in its delicately clear descriptions of the country and of rural
life; in its quaint pastoral scenes, like the interview
with the milkmaid and her mother, and the convo-

cation of gipsies under the hedge; and in its sincerely happy incitements to patience, cheerfulness, a contented spirit, and a tranquil mind.

In its first form the book opened with a dialogue between Piscator and Viator; but later this was revised to a three-sided conversation in which Venator, a hunter, and Auceps, a falconer, take the place of Viator and try valiantly to uphold the merits of their respective sports as superior to angling. Of course Piscator easily gets the best of them, (authors always have this power to reserve victory for their favourites,) and Auceps goes off stage, vanquished, while Venator remains as a convert and willing disciple, to follow his "Master" by quiet streams and drink in his pleasant and profitable discourse. As a dialogue it is not very convincing, it lacks salt and pepper; Venator is too easy a convert; he makes two or three rather neat repartees, but in general he seems to have no mind of his own. But as a monologue it is very agreeable, being written in a sincere, colloquial, unaffected yet not undignified manner, with a plenty of digressions. And these, like the by-paths on a journey, are the pleasantest parts of all. Piscator's talk appears easy, unconstrained, rambling, yet always sure-footed, like the walk of one who has wandered by the little rivers so long that he can move forward safely without watching every step, finding his footing by a kind of instinct while his eyes follow the water and the rising fish.

But we must not imagine that such a style as this, fluent as it seems and easy to read as it is for any one with an ear for music, either comes by nature or is attained without effort. Walton speaks somewhere of his "artless pencil"; but this is true only in the sense that he makes us forget the processes of his art in the simplicity of its results. He was in fact very nice in his selection and ordering of words. He wrote and rewrote his simplest sentences and revised his work in each of the five earlier editions, except possibly the fourth.

Take, for example, the bit which I have already quoted from the "address to the reader" in the first edition, and compare it with the corresponding passage in the fifth edition:

"I am the willinger to justify *the pleasant part of*

it, because, *though it is known I can be serious at reasonable times*, yet the whole discourse is, *or rather was*, a picture of my own disposition, *especially* in such days and times as I *have laid aside business, and gone a-fishing with* honest Nat. and R. Roe; *but they are gone, and with them most of my pleasant hours, even as a shadow that passeth away and returns not*."

All the phrases in italics are either altered or added.

He cites Montaigne's opinion of cats,—a familiar judgment expressed with lightness,—and in the first edition winds up his quotation with the sentence, "To this purpose speaks Montaigne concerning cats." In the fifth edition this is humourously improved to, "Thus *freely* speaks Mountaigne concerning cats,"—as if it were something noteworthy to take a liberty with this petted animal.

The beautiful description of the song of the nightingale, and of the lark, and the fine passage beginning, "Every misery that I miss is a new mercy," are jewels that Walton added in revision.

In the first edition he gravely tells how the salm-

A QUAINT COMRADE

on "will force themselves over the tops of weirs
and hedges or stops in the water, *by taking their
tails into their mouths and leaping over those places,*
even to a height beyond common belief." But
upon reflection this fish-story seems to him dubious; and so in the later edition you find the mouth-
and-tail legend in a poetical quotation, to which
Walton cautiously adds, "*This Michael Drayton
tells you* of this leap or summer-salt of the salmon."

It would be easy to continue these illustrations of
Walton's care in revising his work through successive editions; indeed a long article, or even a little
book might be made upon this subject, and if I had
the time I should like to do it.

Another theme would well repay study, and that
is the influence of the King James Version of the
Bible upon his style and thought. That wonderful
example of pure, strong, and stately English prose,
was first printed and published when Walton was
eighteen years old, about the time he came to London as an apprentice. Yet to such good purpose
did he read and study it that his two books, the
Angler and the *Lives,* are full of apt quotations from

it, and almost every page shows the exemplary effect of its admirable diction. Indeed it has often seemed to me that his fine description of the style of the Prophet Amos, (in the first chapter of the *Angler*,) reveals something of the manner in which Walton himself desired to write; and in this desire he was not altogether unsuccessful.

How clearly the man shines through his book! An honest, kindly man, not ashamed of his trade, nor of his amusements, nor of his inmost faith. A man contented with his modest place in the world, and never doubting that it was a good world or that God made it. A firm man, not without his settled convictions and strong aversions, yet "content that every reader should enjoy his own opinion." A liberal-mannered man, enjoying the music of birds and of merry songs and glees, grateful for good food, and "barly-wine, the good liquor that our honest Fore-fathers did use to drink of," and a fragrant pipe afterwards; sitting down to meat not only with "the eminent clergymen of England," but also, (as his Master did,) with publicans and sinners; and counting among his friends such digni-

taries as Dr. John Hales, Bishop King, and Sir
Henry Wotton, and such lively and vagarious persons as Ben Jonson, Carey, and Charles Cotton.
A loyal, steadfast man, not given to change, anx-
iety of mind, or vain complaining, but holding to
the day's duty and the day's reward of joy as God
sent them to him, and bearing the day's grief with
fortitude. Thus he worked and read and angled
quietly through the stormy years of the Civil War
and the Commonwealth, wishing that men would
beat their swords into fish-hooks, and cast their
leaden bullets into sinkers, and study peace and
the Divine will.

large type, liberal margins, and a-plenty of illustrations. For it is not a book in which economy of bulk is needful; it is less suitable for company on a journey or a fishing-trip, than for a meditative hour in the library after dinner, or a pleasant wakeful hour in bed, when the reading-lamp glows clear and steady, and all the rest of the family are asleep or similarly engaged in recumbent reading.

There are some books with which we can never become intimate. However long we may know them they keep us on the cold threshold of acquaintance. Others boisterously grasp our hand and drag us in, only to bore us and make us regret the day of our introduction. But if there ever was a book which invited genially to friendship and delight it is this of Boswell's. The man who does not know it is ignorant of some of the best cheer that can enliven a solitary fireside. The man who does not enjoy it is insensible alike to the attractions of a noble character vividly depicted, and to the amusement afforded by the sight of a great genius in company with an adoring follower capable, at times, of acting like an engaging ass.

Yet after all, I have always had my doubts about

the supposed "asininity" of Boswell. As his Great
Friend said, "A man who talks nonsense so well
must know that he is talking nonsense." It is only
fair to accept his own explanation and allow that
when he said or did ridiculous things it was, partly
at least, in order to draw out his Tremendous Companion. Thus we may think with pleasure of Boswell taking a rise out of Johnson. But we do not
need to imagine Johnson taking a rise out of Boswell; it was not necessary; he rose of his own ac-
cord. He made a candid record of these diverting
incidents because, though self-complacent, he was
not touchy, and he had sense enough to see that
the sure way to be entirely entertaining is to be
quite frank.

Boswell threw a stone at one bird and brought
down two. His triumphant effort to write the life
of his Immense Hero just as it was, with all its surroundings, appurtenances, and eccentricities, has
won for himself a singular honour: his proper name
has become a common noun. It is hardly necessary to use a capital letter when we allude to a boswell. His pious boast that he had "Johnsonized

the land," is no more correct than it would be to say, (and if he were alive he would certainly say it,) that he had boswellized biography.

The success of the book appears the more remarkable when we remember that of the seventy-five years of Samuel Johnson's life not more than two years and two months were passed in the society of James Boswell. Yet one would almost think that they had been rocked in the same cradle, or, (if this figure of speech seem irreverent,) that the Laird of Auchinleck had slept in a little trundle-bed beside the couch of the Mighty Lexicographer. I do not mean by this that the record is trivial and cubicular, but simply that Boswell has put into his book as much of Johnson as it will hold.

Let no one imagine, however, that a like success can be secured by following the same recipe with any chance subject. The exact portraiture of an insignificant person confers information where there is no curiosity, and becomes tedious in proportion as it is precise.* The first thing needful is to catch

---

* I am haunted by the notion that Johnson himself said this, but I cannot find the passage for quotation.

a giant for your hero; and in this little world it is seldom that one like Johnson comes to the net.

What a man he was,—this "old struggler," as he called himself,—how uncouth and noble and genuine and profound,—"a labouring, working mind; an indolent, reposing body"! What a heart of fortitude in the bosom of his melancholy, what a kernel of human kindness within the shell of his rough manner! He was proud but not vain, sometimes rude but never cruel. His prejudices were insular, but his intellect was continental. There was enough of contradiction in his character to give it variety, and enough of sturdy faith to give it unity. It was not easy for him to be good, but it was impossible for him to be false; and he fought the battle of life through along his chosen line even to the last skirmish of mortality.

I suppose we Americans might harbour a grudge against him on the score of his opinion of our forefathers. It is on record that he said of them, during their little controversy with King George III, that they were "a race of convicts." (How exciting it would have been to hear him say a thing like that

From a photograph, copyright by Hollyer, London.

SAMUEL JOHNSON.
Painted by Reynolds.

to the face of George Washington or Benjamin Franklin! He was quite capable of it.) But we can afford to laugh at such an *obiter dictum* now. And upon my honesty it offends me less at the present time than Lionel Lispingly Nutt's condescending advice on poetry and politics, or Stutterworth Bummell's patronizing half-praise. Let a man smite us fairly on one cheek, and we can manage to turn the other,—out of his reach. But if he deals superciliously with us as "poor relations," we can hardly help looking for a convenient and not too dangerous flight of stairs for his speedy descent.

Johnson may be rightly claimed as a Tory-Democrat on the strength of his serious saying that "the interest of millions must ever prevail over that of thousands," and the temper of his pungent letter to Lord Chesterfield. And when we consider also his side remark in defense of card-playing on the ground that it "generates kindness and consolidates society," we may differ from him in our estimate of the game, but we cannot deny that in small things as well as in great he spoke as a liberal friend of humanity.

His literary taste was not infallible; in some instances, (for example his extreme laudation of Sir John Denham's poem *Cooper's Hill,* and his adverse criticism of Milton's verse,) it was very bad. In general you may say that it was based upon theories and rules which are not really of universal application, though he conceived them to be so. But his style was much more the product of his own personality and genius. Ponderous it often was, but seldom clumsy. He had the art of saying what he meant in a deliberate, clear, forceful way. Words arrayed themselves at his command and moved forward in serried phalanx. He had the praiseworthy habit of completing his sentences and building his paragraphs firmly. It will not do us any good to belittle his merit as a writer, particularly in this age of slipper-shod and dressing-gowned English.

His diction was much more varied than people usually suppose. He could suit his manner to almost any kind of subject, except possibly the very lightest. He had a keen sense of the shading of synonyms and rarely picked the wrong word. Of antithesis and the balanced sentence he was over-fond; and this device, intended originally to give a sharpened emphasis, being used too often, lends an air of monotony to his writing. Yet it has its merits too, as may be seen in these extracts from the fiftieth number of *The Rambler*,—extracts which, by the way, have some relation to a controversy still raging:

"Every old man complains of the growing depravity of the world, of the petulance and insolence of the rising generation. He recounts the decency and regularity of former times, and celebrates the discipline and sobriety of the age in which his youth was passed; a happy age, which is now no more to be expected, since confusion has broken in upon the world and thrown down all the boundaries of civility and reverence. . . . It may, therefore, very reasonably be suspected that the old draw upon themselves the greatest part of those insults which they so much lament, and that age is rarely despised but when it is contemptible. . . . He that would pass the latter part of his life with honour and decency, must, when he is young, consider that he shall one day be old; and remember, when he is old, that he has once been young. In youth, he must lay up knowledge for his support, when his powers of action shall forsake him; and in age forbear to animadvert with rigour on faults which experience only can correct."

In meaning this is very much the same as Sir James Barrie's recent admirable discourse on "Courage" at the University of St. Andrew's; but in manner there is quite a difference.

It is commonly supposed that Dr. Johnson did a great deal to overload and oppress the English language by introducing new and awkward words of monstrous length. His opportunities in that way were large, but he always claimed that he had used them with moderation and had not coined above four or five words. When we note that "peregrinity" was one of them, we are grateful that he refrained so much; but when we remember that "clubbable" was another, we are glad that he did not refrain altogether. For there is no quality more easy to recognize and difficult to define than that which makes a man acceptable in a club; and of this Dr. Johnson has given us a fine example in his life and an appropriate name in his word.

318

A STURDY BELIEVER

I think one reason why he got on so well with people who differed from him, and why most of the sensible ones so readily put up with his downright and often brusque way of expressing his sentiments, was because they came so evidently from his sincere and unshakeable conviction that certain things are true, that they can not be changed, and that they should not be forgotten. Not only in politics, but also and more significantly in religion, Samuel Johnson stands out as a sturdy believer.

This seems the more noteworthy when we consider the conditions of his life. There is hardly one among the great men of history who can be called so distinctively "a man of letters," undoubtedly none who has won as high a position and as large a contemporary influence by sheer strength of pen. Now the literary life is not generally considered to be especially favourable to the cultivation of religion; and Johnson's peculiar circumstances were not of a kind to make it more favourable in his case than usual. He was poor and neglected, struggling during a great part of his career against the heaviest odds. His natural disposition was by no means such as to predispose him to faith. He was afflicted

319

from childhood with a hypochondriac and irritable humour; a high, domineering spirit, housed in an unwieldy and disordered body; plagued by inordinate physical appetites; inclined naturally to rely with over-confidence upon the strength and accuracy of his reasoning powers; driven by his impetuous temper into violent assertion and controversy; deeply depressed by his long years of obscurity and highly elated by his final success,—he was certainly not one whom we would select as likely to be a remarkably religious man. Carlyle had less to embitter him. Goethe had no more to excuse self-idolatry. And yet, beyond a doubt, Johnson was a sincere, humble, and, in the main, a consistent Christian.

Of course, we cannot help seeing that his peculiarities and faults affected his religion. He was intolerant in his expression of theological views to a degree which seems almost ludicrous. We may, perhaps, keep a straight face and a respectful attitude when we see him turning his back on the Abbé Raynal, and refusing to "shake hands with an infidel." But when he exclaims in regard to a young lady who had left the Church of England to become a Quaker, "I hate the wench and shall ever hate her; I hate all impudence of a chit; apostasy I nauseate"; and when he answers the gently expressed hope of a friend that he and the girl would meet, after all, in a blessed eternity, by saying, "Madam, I am not fond of *meeting fools anywhere*," we cannot help joining in the general laughter of the company to whom he speaks; and as the Doctor himself finally laughs and becomes cheerful and entertaining, we feel that it was only the bear in him that growled,—an honest beast, but sometimes very surly.

As for his remarkable strictures upon Presbyterianism, his declaration that he preferred the Roman Catholic Church, his expressed hope that John Knox was buried in the highway, and his wish that a dangerous steeple in Edinburgh might not be taken down because if it were let alone it might fall on some of the posterity of John Knox, which, he said, would be "no great matter,"—if when we read these things we remember that he was talking to his Scotch friend Boswell, we get a new idea of the audacity of the great man's humour. I believe he even stirred up his natural high-churchism to rise rampant and roar vigourously, for the pleasure of seeing Boswell's eyes stand out, and his neat little pigtail vibrate in dismay.

There are many other sayings of Johnson's which disclose a deeper vein of tolerance; such as that remark about the essential agreement and trivial differences of all Christians, and his warm commendation, on his dying bed, of the sermons of Dr. Samuel Clarke, a Dissenting minister.

But even suppose we are forced to admit that Dr. Johnson was lacking in that polished liberality, that willingness to admit that every other man's opinions are as good as his own, which we have come nowadays to regard as the chief of the theological virtues; even suppose we must call him "narrow," we must admit at the same time that he was "deep"; he had a profundity of conviction, a sincerity of utterance which made of his religion something, as the Germans say, "to take hold of with your hands."

He had need of a sturdy belief. With that tempestuous, unruly disposition of his boiling all the

occasions and with due respect." He approached
the consideration of divine things with genuine solemnity, and could not tolerate sacred trifling or
pious profanity. He was not ashamed to kneel
where men could see him, although he never courted
their notice; or to pray where men could hear him,
although he did not desire their approbation any
more than he feared their ridicule.

There were grave faults and errors in his conduct.
But no one had so keen a sense of their unworthiness
as the man himself, who was bravely fighting against
them, and sincerely lamenting their recurrence.
They often tripped him and humiliated him, but
they never got him completely down. He righted
himself and went lumbering on. He never sold his
heart to a lie, never confused the evil and the good.
When he sinned he knew it and repented. It gives
us confidence in his sincerity when we see him deny-
ing himself the use of wine because he was naturally
prone to excess, and yet allowing it to his friends
who were able to use it temperately. He was no
puritan; and, on the other hand, he was no slipshod condoner of vice or suave preacher of moral

327

indifference. He was a big, honest soul, trying hard to live straight along the line of duty and to do good as he found opportunity.

The kindness and generosity of his heart were known to few save his intimate friends, and not always appreciated even by those who had most cause to be grateful to him. The poor broken-down pensioners with whom he filled his house in later years, and to whom he alluded playfully as his *seraglio*, were a constant source of annoyance. They grumbled perpetually and fought like so many cats. But he would not cast them off any more than he would turn out his favourite mouser, Hodge, for whom he used to "go out and buy oysters, lest the servants having that trouble should take a dislike to the poor creature." He gave away a large part of his income in charity; and, what was still more generous, he devoted a considerable portion of his time to counseling young and unsuccessful authors and, (note this,) *reading their manuscripts*.

I suppose if one had been a poverty-stricken beginner at literature, in London of the eighteenth century, the best thing one could have done would have been to find the way to Dr. Johnson's house and tell him how the case stood. If he himself had no money to lend, he would have borrowed it from some of his friends. And if he could not say anything encouraging about the manuscripts, he would have been honest and kind enough to advise the unhappy aspirant to fame to prefer the life of a competent shoemaker to that of an incompetent scribbler.

Much of what was best in the character of Johnson came out in his friendships. He was as good a lover as he was a hater. He was loyal to a fault, and sincere, though never extravagant, in his admirations.

The picture of the old man in his last illness, surrounded by the friends whom he had cherished so faithfully, and who now delighted to testify their respect and affection for him, and brighten his lingering days with every attention, has little of the customary horror of a death-bed. It is strange indeed that he who had always been subject to such a dread of dying should have found it possible to meet the hour of dissolution with such composure.

His old friend Sir Joshua Reynolds comes in to bid him farewell, and Johnson makes three requests of him,—to forgive him thirty pounds which he had borrowed from him, to read the Bible, and never to use his pencil on a Sunday. Good petitions, which Sir Joshua readily granted, although we cannot help fearing that he occasionally forgot the last.

"Tell me," says the sick man to his physician, "can I possibly recover? Give me a direct answer." Being hard pressed, Dr. Brocklesby confesses that in his opinion recovery is out of the question. "Then," says Johnson, "I will take no more physick, not even my opiates: for I have prayed that I may render up my soul to God unclouded."

And so with kind and thoughtful words to his servant, and a "God bless you, my dear" to the young daughter of a friend who stood lingering at the door of his room, this sturdy old believer went out to meet the God whom he had tried so honestly to serve. His life was an amazing victory over poverty, sickness, and sin. Greatness alone could not have insured, nor could perseverance alone have commanded, three of his good fortunes in this world: that Sir Joshua Reynolds painted his portrait; that Boswell wrote his biography; and that HIS WIFE said of him that "he was the most sensible man she had ever met."

A PURITAN PLUS POETRY

A PURITAN PLUS POETRY

I

A FRIEND of mine, one of the Elder Bookmen of Harvard, told me some twenty years ago that he had only once seen Ralph Waldo Emerson vexed out of his transcendental tranquillity and almost Olympian calm. It was a Sunday afternoon in Concord, and the philosopher had been drawn from his study by an unwonted noise in the house. On the back porch he found his own offspring and some children of the neighbours engaged in a romping, boisterous game. With visible anger he stopped it, saying, "Even if you have no reverence for the day, you ought to have enough sense and manners to respect the traditions of your forefathers."

Emerson's puritanism was in the blood. Seven of his ancestors were ministers of New England churches of the early type. Among them was Peter

Bulkley, who left his comfortable parish in Bedfordshire, England, to become the pastor of "the church in the wilderness" at Concord, Massachusetts; Father Samuel Moody of Agamenticus, Maine, who was such a zealous reformer that he pursued wayward sinners even into the alehouse to reprove them; Joseph Emerson of Malden, a "heroic scholar," who prayed every night that no descendant of his might ever be rich; and William Emerson, the patriot preacher, who died while serving in the army of the Revolution. These were verily "soldiers of the Lord," and from them and women of like stamina and mettle, Emerson inherited the best of puritan qualities: independence, sobriety, fearless loyalty to conscience, strenuous and militant virtue.

But he had also a super-gift which was not theirs. That which made him different from them, gave him a larger and more beautiful vision of the world, led him into ways of thinking and speaking which to them would have seemed strange and perilous, (though in conduct he followed the strait and narrow path,)—in short, that which made him what he was in himself and to countless other men, a seer, an inspirer, a singer of new light and courage and joy, was the gift of poetic imagination and interpretation. He was a puritan *plus* poetry.

Graduating from Harvard he began life as a teacher in a Boston school and afterwards the minister of a Boston church. But there was something in his temperament which unfitted him for the service of institutions. He was a servant of ideas. To do his best work he needed to feel himself entirely independent of everything except allegiance to the truth as God gave him to see it from day to day. The scholastic routine of a Female Academy irked him. The social distinctions and rivalries of city life appeared to him both insincere and tiresome. Even the mild formulas and regulations of a Unitarian church seemed to hamper him. He was a come-outer; he wished to think for himself, to proclaim his own visions, to act and speak only from the inward impulse, though always with an eye to the good of others. So he left his parish in Boston and became a preacher at large to "these United States." His pulpit was the lecture-platform; his little books of prose and verse carried his words to a still larger audience; no man in America during his life had a more extended or a deeper influence; he became famous both as an orator and as a writer; but in fact he was always preaching. As Lamb said to Coleridge, "I never heard you do anything else."

The central word of all his discourse is Self-reliance,—be yourself, trust yourself, and fear not! But in order to interpret this rightly one must have at least an inkling of his philosophy, which was profoundly religious and essentially poetical. He was a mystic, an intuitional thinker. He believed that the whole universe of visible things is only a kind of garment which covers the real world of invisible ideas and laws and principles. He believed also that each man, having a share in the Divine Reason which is the source of all things, may have a direct knowledge of truth through his own innate ideas and intuitive perceptions. Emerson wrote in his diary, "The highest revelation is that God is in every man."

This way of thinking is called transcendentalism, because it overleaps logic and scientific reasoning.

It is easy to see how such a philosophy might lead unbalanced persons into wild and queer and absurd views and practices. And so it did when it struck the neighbourhood of Boston in the second quarter of the 19th Century, and began to spread from that sacred centre.

But with these vagaries Emerson had little sympathy. His mysticism was strongly tinctured with common sense, (which also is of divine origin,) and his orderly nature recoiled from eccentric and irregular ways. Although for a time he belonged to the "Transcendental Club," he frequently said that he would not be called a transcendentalist, and at times he made fun, in a mild and friendly spirit, of the extreme followers of that doctrine. He held as strongly as any one that the Divine light of reason in each man is the guide to truth; but he held it with the important reservation that when this inner light really shines, free from passion and prejudice, it will never lead a man away from good judgment and the moral law. All through his life he navigated the transcendental sea safely, piloted by a puritan conscience, warned off the rocks by a keen sense of humour, and kept from capsizing by a solid ballast of New England prudence.

He was in effect one of the most respected, sagacious, prosperous and virtuous villagers of Concord. Some slight departures from common custom he tranquilly tested and as tranquilly abandoned. He tried vegetarianism for a while, but gave it up when he found that it did him no good. He attempted to introduce domestic democracy by having the servants sit at table with the rest of the household, but was readily induced to abandon the experiment by the protest of his two sensible hired girls against such an inconvenient arrangement. He began to practise a theory that manual labour should form part of the scholar's life, but was checked by the personal discovery that hard work in the garden meant poor work in the study. "The writer shall not dig," was his conclusion. Intellectual freedom was what he chiefly desired; and this he found could best be attained in an inconspicuous manner of living and dressing, not noticeably different from that of the average college professor or country minister.

Here you see the man "in his habit as he lived,"

From a photograph by Black, Boston.

RALPH WALDO EMERSON.

(and as thousands of lecture-audiences saw him,) pictured in the old photograph which illustrates this chapter. Here is the familiar *décor* of the photographer's studio: the curtain draped with a cord and tassel, the muslin screen background, and probably that hidden instrument of torture, the "head-rest," behind the tall, posed figure. Here are the solemn "swallow-tail coat," the conventional cravat, and the black satin waistcoat. Yet even this antique "carte de visite," it seems to me, suggests something more and greater,—the imperturbable, kindly presence, the noble face, the angelic look, the serene manner, the penetrating and revealing quality of the man who set out to be "a friend to all who wished to live in the spirit."

Whatever the titles of his lectures,—*Man the Reformer, The Method of Nature, The Conduct of Life, Fate, Compensation, Prudence, The Present Age, Society and Solitude,*—his main theme is always the same, "namely the infinitude of the private man." But this private man of Emerson's, mark you, is linked by invisible ties to all Nature and carries in his breast a spark of the undying fire which is of

God. Hence he is at his best when he feels not only his personal *unity* but also his universal *community*, when he relies on himself and at the same time cries

"I yield myself to the perfect whole."

This kind of independence is the truest form of obedience.

The charm of Emerson's way of presenting his thought comes from the spirit of poetry in the man. He does not argue, nor threaten, nor often exhort; he reveals what he has seen or heard, for you to make what you will of it. He relies less on syllogisms than on imagery, symbols, metaphors. His utterance is as inspirational as the ancient oracle of Delphi, but he shuns the contortions of the priestess at that shrine.

The clearness and symmetry of his sentences, the modulations of his thrilling voice, the radiance of his fine features and his understanding smile, even his slight hesitations and pauses over his manuscript as he read, lent a singular attraction to his speech. Those who were mistrustful of his views on theology and the church, listened to him with delight when he poetized on art, politics, literature, human society and the natural world. To the finest men and women of America in the mid-Victorian epoch he was the lecturer *par excellence*, the intellectual awakener and liberator, the messenger calling them to break away from dull, thoughtless, formal ways of doing things, and live freely in harmony with the laws of God and their own spirit. They heard him gladly.

I wonder how he would fare today, when lecturers, male or female, have to make a loud noise to get a hearing.

II

Emerson's books, prose and verse, remain with us and still live,—"the precious life-blood of a masterspirit, embalmed and treasured up on purpose to a life beyond life." That they are companionable is proved by the way all sorts of companionable people love them. I know a Pullman car conductor who swears by Emerson. A young French Canadian woodsman, (who is going to work his way through college,) told me the other day that he liked Emerson's essays better than any other English book that he had read. Restive girls and boys of the "new generation" find something in him which appeals to them; reading farmers of New England and the West prefer him to Plato; even academic professors and politicians qualifying for statesmen feel his stimulating and liberating influence, although (or perhaps because) he sometimes says such hard things about them. I guess that nothing yet written in America is likely to live longer than Emerson's best work.

His prose is better known and more admired than his verse, for several reasons: first, because he took more pains to make the form of it as perfect as he could; second, because it has a wider range and an easier utterance; third, because it has more touches of wit and of familiarity with the daily doings of men; and finally, because the majority of readers probably prefer prose for silent reading, since the full charm of good verse is revealed only in reading aloud.

But for all that, with Emerson, (as with a writer

so different as Matthew Arnold,) I find something in the poems which is not in the essays,—a more pure and subtle essence of what is deepest in the man. Poetry has a power of compression which is beyond prose. It says less and suggests more.

Emerson wrote to the girl whom he afterwards married: "I am born a poet,—of a low class without doubt, but a poet. . . . My singing, to be sure, is very husky and is for the most part in prose. Still I am a poet in the sense of a perceiver and dear lover of the harmonies that are in the soul and in matter, and specially of the correspondence between them." This is penetrating self-criticism. That he was "of a low class" as poet is more than doubtful,—an error of modesty. But that his singing was often "husky" cannot be denied. He never troubled himself to learn the art of song. The music of verse, in which Longfellow gained such mastery, and Lowell and Whittier had such native gifts, is not often found in Emerson's poetry. His measures rarely flow with freedom and harmony. They are alternately stiff and spasmodic, and the rhymes are sometimes threadbare, sometimes eccentric.

Many of his poems are so condensed, so tight-packed with thought and information that they seem to labour along like an overladen boat in a choppy sea. For example, this:

> "The journeying atoms,
> Primordial wholes,
> Firmly draw, firmly drive,
> By their animate poles."

Or this:

> "Puny man and scentless rose
> Tormenting Pan to double the dose."

But for these defects of form Emerson as poet makes ample amends by the richness and accuracy of his observation of nature, by the vigorous flight of his imagination, by the depth and at times the passionate controlled intensity of his feeling. Of love-poetry he has none, except the philosophical. Of narrative poetry he has practically none, unless you count such brief, vivid touches as,—

> "By the rude bridge that arched the flood,
> Their flag to April's breeze unfurled,
> Here once the embattled farmers stood,
> And fired the shot heard round the world."

But his descriptive pieces are of a rare beauty and charm. truthful in broad outline and delicate detail, every flower and every bird in its right colour and place.   Walking with him you see and breathe New England in the light of early morn, with the dew sparkling on the grass and all the cosmic forces working underneath it.   His reflective and symbolic poems, like *Each and All*, *The Problem*, *Forerunners*, *Days*, *The Sphinx*, are full of a searching and daring imaginative power.   He has also the genius of the perfect phrase.

"The frolic architecture of the snow."

"Earth proudly wears the Parthenon,
As the best gem upon her zone"

"The silent organ loudest chants
The Master's requiem."

"Music pours on mortals
Its beautiful disdain."

"Over the winter glaciers,
I see the summer glow,
And through the wild-piled snowdrift
The warm rose-buds below."

"I thenceforward and long after,
Listen for their harp-like laughter,
And carry in my heart, for days,
Peace that hallows rudest ways."

His *Threnody*, written after the early death of his first-born son, has always seemed to me one of the most moving elegies in the English tongue. His patriotic poems, especially the *Concord Ode*, are unsurpassed as brief, lyrical utterances of the spirit of America. In certain moods, when the mind is in vigour and the windows of far vision open at a touch, Emerson's small volume of *Poems* is a most companionable book.

As his prose sometimes intrudes into his verse and checks its flow, so his poetry often runs over into his prose and illuminates it. What could be more poetic in conception than this sentence from his first book, *Nature?* "If the stars should appear but one night in a thousand years, how would men believe and adore and preserve for many generations the remembrance of the city of God which had been shown!"

Emerson's *Essays* are a distillation of his lectures. His way of making these was singular and all his own. It was his habit to keep note-books in which he jotted down bits of observation about nature,

348

stray thoughts and comparisons, reflections on his reading, and striking phrases which came to him in meditation or talk. Choosing a subject he planted it in his mind and waited for ideas and illustrations to come to it, as birds or insects to a flower. When a thought appeared he followed it, "as a boy might hunt a butterfly," and when it was captured he pinned it in his "thought-book." No doubt there were mental laws at work all the time, giving guidance and direction to the process of composition which seemed so irregular and haphazard. There is no lack of vital unity in one of Emerson's lectures or essays. It deals with a single subject and never gets really out of sight of the proposition with which it begins. Yet it seldom gives a complete, all-round view of it. It is more like a series of swift and vivid glimpses of the same object seen from different stand-points, a collection of snap-shot pictures taken in the course of a walk around some great mountain.

From the pages of his note-books he gathered the material for one of his lectures, selecting and arranging it under some such title as Fate, Genius, Beauty, Manners, Duty, The Anglo-Saxon, The Young

American, and giving it such form and order as he thought would be most effective in delivery. If the lecture was often repeated, (as it usually was,) the material was frequently rearranged, the pages were shifted, the illustrations changed. Then, after it had served its purpose, the material was again rearranged and published in a volume of *Essays*.

It is easy to trace in the essays the effects of this method of writing. The material is drawn from a wide range of reading and observation. Emerson is especially fond of poetry, philosophy and books of anecdote and biography. He quotes from Shakespeare, Dante, Goethe, George Herbert, Wordsworth, Plutarch, Grimm, St. Simon, Swedenborg, Behmen the mystic, Plato, and the religious books of the East. His illustrations come from far and near. Now they are strange and remote, now homely and familiar. The Zodiac of Denderah; the Savoyards who carved their pine-forests into toys; the *lustrum* of silence which Pythagoras made his disciples keep; Napoleon on the *Bellerophon* watching the drill of the English soldiers; the Egyptian legend that every man has two pair of eyes; Empedocles and his shoe; the flat strata of the earth; a soft mushroom pushing up through the hard ground; —all these allusions and a hundred more are found in the same volume. On his pages, close beside the Parthenon, St. Paul's, the Sphinx, Ætna and Vesuvius, you will read of the White Mountains, Monadnock, Katahdin, the pickerel-weed in bloom, the wild geese honking across the sky, the chickadee singing in the face of winter, the Boston State-house, Wall Street, cotton-mills, railroads, Quincy granite, and so forth. Nothing is too far away to seem real to him, nothing too near to seem interesting and valuable. There is an abundance, sometimes a superabundance, of material in his essays, not always well-assorted, but all vivid and suggestive.

The structure of the essay, the way of putting the material together, does not follow any fixed rule or system. Yet in most cases it has a well-considered and suitable form; it stands up; it is architecturally built, though the art is concealed. I once amused myself trying to analyze some of the essays, and found that many of the best ones have a definite theme, like a text, and follow a regular plan of development, with introduction, discussion, and conclusion. In some cases Emerson does not disdain the "heads and horns" of the old-fashioned preacher, and numbers his points "first," "second," "third," —perhaps even "fourth." But this is rare. For the most part the essays do not seem to be constructed but to grow. They are like conversations with the stupid things left out. They turn aside from dull points, and omit connecting links, and follow an attractive idea wherever it may lead. They seldom exhaust a subject, but they usually illuminate it.

"The style is the man," and in this case it is well suited to his material and his method. It is brilliant, sparkling, gemlike. He has great freedom in the choice of words, using them sometimes in odd ways and not always correctly. Generally his diction is made up of terse, pungent Anglo-Saxon phrases, but now and then he likes to bring in a stately word of Greek or Latin origin, with a telling effect of contrast. Most of his sentences are short and clear; it is only in the paragraph that he is sometimes cloudy. Every essay is rich in epigrams.

A PURITAN PLUS POETRY

If one reads too much of a style like this, the effect becomes fatiguing. You miss the long, full, steady flow of sentences with varied cadence and changing music.

Emerson's river is almost all rapids. The flash and sparkle of phrase after phrase tire me after a while. But for a short voyage nothing could be more animated and stimulating. I read one essay at a time and rise refreshed.

But the secret of Emerson's power, (to change the figure,) is in the wine which he offers, not the cup into which he pours it. His great word,—"self-reliance,"—runs through all his writing and pervades all that he says. At times it is put in an extreme form, and might lead, if rashly followed, to intellectual conceit and folly. But it is balanced by other words, no less potent,—self-criticism, modesty, consideration, prudence, and reverence. He is an aspiring, hopeful teacher of youth; correcting follies with a sharp wit; encouraging noble ambitions; making the face of nature luminous with the glow of poetic imagination; and elevating life with an ideal patriotism and a broad humanity. In all his writing one feels the serene, lofty influence of a sane and chastened optimism, the faith which holds, amid many appearances which are dark, mysterious and terrifying, that Good is stronger than Evil and will triumph at last everywhere.

Read what he says in the essay called *Compensation*: "There is no penalty to virtue; no penalty to wisdom; they are proper additions of being. In a virtuous action I properly *am;* in a virtuous act I add to the world; I plant into deserts conquered from Chaos and Nothing, and see the darkness receding on the limits of the horizon. There can be no excess to love, none to knowledge, none to beauty, when these attributes are considered in the purest sense. The soul refuses limits, and always affirms an Optimism, never a Pessimism."

This is the note that brings a brave joy to the ear of youth. Old age gladly listens to the same note in the deeper, quieter music of Emerson's poem, *Terminus.*

> "As the bird trims her to the gale,
> I trim myself to the storm of time,
> I man the rudder, reef the sail,

Obey the voice at eve obeyed at prime:
'Lowly faithful, banish fear,
Right onward drive unharmed;
The port, well worth the cruise, is near,
And every wave is charmed.'"

AN ADVENTURER IN A VELVET
JACKET

AN ADVENTURER IN A VELVET JACKET

THUS gallantly he appears in my mind's eye when I pause in rereading one of his books and summon up a fantasm of the author,—Robert Louis Stevenson, gentleman adventurer in life and letters, his brown eyes shining in a swarthy face, his lean, long-enduring body adorned with a black-velvet jacket.

This garment is no disguise but a symbol. It is short, so as not to impede him with entangling tails. It is unconventional, as a protest against the tyranny of fashion. But it is of velvet, mark you, to match a certain niceness of choice and preference of beauty, —yes, and probably a touch of bravura,—in all its wearer's vagaries. 'Tis like the silver spurs, broad sombrero and gay handkerchief of the thoroughbred cowboy,—not an element of the dandiacal, but a tribute to romance. Strange that the most genuine of men usually have a bit of this in their composition; your only incurable *poseur* being the fellow

359

who affects never to pose and betrays himself by
his attitude of scorn.

Of course, Stevenson did not always wear this
symbolic garment. In fact the only time I met
him in the flesh his clothes had a discouraging resemblance to those of the rest of us at the Authors
Club in New York. And a few months ago, when
I traced his "footprints on the sands of time" at
Waikiki beach, near Honolulu, the picture drawn
for me by those who knew him when he passed that
way, was that of a lank, bare-footed, bright-eyed,
sun-browned man who daundered along the shore
in white-duck trousers and a shirt wide open at the
neck. But the velvet jacket was in his wardrobe,
you may be sure, ready for fitting weather and occasion. He wore it, very likely, when he went to
beard the Honolulu colourman who was trying to
"do" his stepson-in-law in the matter of a bill for
paints. He put it on when he banqueted with his
amiable but bibulous friend, King Kalakaua. You
can follow it through many, if not most, of the pho-
tographs which he had taken from his twentieth to
his forty-fourth, and last, year. And in his style

From a photograph, negative of which is owned by Charles Scribner's Sons.

ROBERT LOUIS STEVENSON.

you can almost always feel it,—the touch of distinction, the ease of a native elegance, the assurance of a well-born wanderer,—in short, the velvet jacket.

Robert Lewis Balfour Stevenson began the adventure of life in a decent little house in Howard Place, Edinburgh, on November 13, 1850. He completed it on the Samoan island of Upolu in the South Seas, December 3, 1894,—completed it, I think, for though he left his work unfinished he had arrived at the port of honour and the haven of happy rest.

His father, and his father's father, were engineers connected with the Board of Northern Lights. This sounds like being related to the Aurora Borealis; and indeed there was something of mystery and magic about Stevenson, as if an influence from that strange midnight dawn had entered his blood. But as a matter of fact the family occupation was nothing more uncanny than that of building and maintaining lighthouses and beacons along the Scottish coast, a profession in which they won considerable renown and to which the lad himself was originally assigned. He made a fair try at it, and even won a silver medal for an essay on improvements in lighthouses. But the calling did not suit him, and he said afterward that he gained little from it except "properties for some possible romance, or words to add to my vocabulary."

This lanky, queer, delicate, headstrong boy was a dreamer of dreams, and from youth desperately fond of writing. He felt himself a predestinated author, and like a true Scot toiled diligently to make his calling and election sure.

But there was one thing for which he cared more than for writing, and that was living. He plunged into it eagerly, with more zest than wisdom, trying all the games that cities offer, and learning some rather disenchanting lessons at a high price. For in truth neither his physical, nor (as he later discovered) his moral, nature was suited to the sowing of wild oats. His constitution was one of the frailest ever exposed to the biting winds and soaking mists of the North British Boston. Early death seemed to be written in his horoscope. But an indomitable spirit laughs at dismal predictions. Robert Louis

Stevenson, (as he now called himself, velvet-jacketing his own name,) was not the man to be easily snuffed out by weak lungs or wild weather. Mocking at "bloody Jack" he held fast to life with grim, cheerful, grotesque courage; his mother, his wife, his trusty friends, heartened him for the combat; and he succeeded in having a wider experience and doing more work than falls to the lot of many men in rudely exuberant health. To do this calls for a singular kind of bravery, not inferior to, nor unlike, that of the good soldier who walks with Death undismayed.

Undoubtedly Stevenson was born with a *Wanderlust*.

> " My mistress was the open road
> And the bright eyes of danger."

Ill health gave occasion and direction to many voyages and experiments, some of which bettered him, while others made him worse. As a bachelor he roamed mountains afoot and travelled rivers in his own boat, explored the purlieus and sublittorals of Paris, London, and Edinburgh, lodged "on the seacoast of Bohemia," crossed the ocean as an emigrant, and made himself vagrantly at home in California where he married the wife "the great Artificer made for him." They passed their honeymoon in a deserted miner's cabin, and then lived around, in Scotland, the Engadine, Southern France, Bournemouth, the Adirondacks, and on a schooner among the South Sea Islands, bringing up at last in the pleasant haven of Vailima. On all these distant roads Death pursued him, and, till the last ten years, Poverty was his companion. Yet he looked with keen and joyful eyes upon the changing face of the world and into its shadowy heart without trembling. He kept his spirit unbroken, his faith unquenched even when the lights burned low. He counted life

> "just a stuff
> To try the soul's strength on and educe the man."

He may have stumbled and sometimes fallen, things may have looked black to him; but he never gave up, and in spite of frailties and burdens, he travelled a long way,—upward. Through all his travels and tribulations he kept on writing, writing, writing,— the very type of a migratory author. He made his first appearance in a canoe. The log of this journey, *An Inland Voyage on French Rivers*, published in 1878, was a modest, whimsical, charming début in literature. In 1879 he appeared again, and this time with a quaint companion. *Travels with a Donkey in the Cevennes* is one of the most delightful, uninstructive descriptions of a journey ever written in English. It contains no practical information but plenty of pleasure and profit. I do not envy the reader who can finish it without loving that obstinate little mouse-coloured Modestine, and feeling that she is one of the best-drawn female characters, of her race, in fiction.

From this good, quiet beginning his books followed rapidly, and (after *Treasure Island*, that incomparable boys' book for men,) with growing popularity among the judicious, the "gentle readers," who choose books not because they are recommended by professors or advertised in department stores, but because they are really well written and worth reading.

It is difficult to classify Stevenson's books, perhaps just because they are migrants, borderers.

Yet I think a rough grouping, at least of his significant works, may be made. There are five volumes
of travels; six or seven volumes of short stories;
nine longer novels or romances; three books of verse;
three books of essays; one biography; and one
study of South Sea politics. This long list lights
up two vital points in the man: his industry and
his versatility.

"A virtue and a vice," say you? Well, that may
be as you choose to take it, reader. But if you say
it in a sour or a puritanical spirit, Stevenson will
gaily contradict you, making light of what you
praise and vaunting what you blame.

Industry? Nonsense! Did he not write *An
Apology for Idlers?* Yet unquestionably he was a
toiler; his record proves it. Fleeing from one land
to another to shake off his implacable enemy; camp-
ing briefly in strange places; often laid on his back
by sickness and sometimes told to "move on" by
Policeman Penury; collecting his books by post and
correcting his proofs in bed; he made out to produce twenty-nine volumes in sixteen years,—say
8,000 pages of 300 words, each,—a thing manifestly
impossible without a mort of work. But of this he

thought less than of the fact that he did it, as a rule, cheerfully and with a high heart. Herein he came near to his own ideal of success: "To be honest, to be kind—to earn a little and to spend a little less, to make upon the whole a family happier for his presence, to renounce when that shall be necessary and not to be embittered, to keep a few friends, but these without capitulation,—above all, on the same grim condition, to keep friends with himself—here is a task for all that a man has of fortitude and delicacy." Of his work I think he would have said that he stuck to it, first, because he needed the money that it brought in, and second, because he enjoyed it exceedingly. With this he would have smiled away the puritan who wished to pat him on the back for industry.

That he was versatile, turned from one subject to another, tried many forms of his art, and succeeded in some better than in others, he would have admitted boldly—even before those critics who speak slightingly of versatility as if it marked some inferiority in a writer, whereas they dislike it chiefly because it gives them extra trouble in putting him into his precise pigeonhole of classification. Stevenson would have referred these gentlemen to his masters Scott and Thackeray for a justification. His versatility was not that of a weathercock whirled about by every wind of literary fashion, but that of a well-mounted gun which can be turned towards any mark. He did not think that because he had struck a rich vein of prose story-telling he must follow that lead until he had worked it or himself out. He was a prospector as well as a miner. He wished to roam around, to explore things, books, and men, to see life vividly as it is, and then to write what he thought of it in any form that seemed to him fit,—essay, or story, or verse. And this he did, thank God, without misgiving, and on the whole greatly to our benefit and enjoyment.

I am writing now of the things which make his books companionable. That is why I have begun with a thumb-nail sketch of the man in the velvet jacket who lives in them and in his four volumes of letters,—the best English letters, it seems to me, since Lamb and Thackeray. That also is why I have not cared to interrupt this simple essay by telling which of his works strike me as comparative failures, and giving more or less convincing reasons why certain volumes in my "collective edition" are less worn than others.

'Tis of these others that I wish to speak,—the volumes whose bindings are like a comfortable suit of old clothes and on whose pages there are pencil-marks like lovers' initials cut upon the bark of friendly trees. What charm keeps them alive and fresh, in an age when most books five years old are considered out of date and everything from the un-spacious times of Queen Victoria is cordially damned? What manner of virility is in them to evoke, and to survive, such a flood of "Steven-soniana"? What qualities make them still wel-come to so wide a range of readers, young and old, simple and learned,—yes, even among that fair and capricious sex whose claim to be courted his earlier writings seem so lightly (or prudently) to neglect?

I

Over and above the attraction of his pervading personality, I think the most obvious charm of Stevenson's books lies in the clear, vivid, accurate and strong English in which they are written. Reading them is like watching a good golfer drive or putt the ball with clean strokes in which energy is never wanting and never wasted. He does not foozle, or lose his temper in a hazard, or brandish his brassy like a war-club. There is a grace of freedom in his play which comes from practice and self-control.

Stevenson describes (as far as such a thing is possible) the way in which he got his style. "All through my boyhood and youth," says he, "I was known and pointed out for the pattern of an idler, and yet I was always busy on my own private end, which was to learn to write." He traces with gusto, and doubtless with as much accuracy as can be expected in a map drawn from memory, the trails of early admiration which he followed towards this goal. His list of "authors whom I have imitated" is most entertaining: Hazlitt, Lamb, Wordsworth, Sir Thomas Browne, Defoe, Hawthorne, Montaigne, Baudelaire, Obermann. In another essay, on "Books Which Have Influenced Me," he names *The Bible*, *Hamlet*, *As You Like It*, *King Lear*, *Le Vicomte de Bragelonne*, *The Pilgrim's Progress*, *Leaves of Grass*, Herbert Spencer's books, Lewes's *Life of Goethe*, the *Meditations* of Marcus Aurelius, the poems of Wordsworth, George Meredith's *The Egoist*, the essays of Thoreau and Hazlitt, Mitford's *Tales of Old Japan*,—a strange catalogue, but not incoherent if you remember that he is speaking now more of their effect upon his way of thinking than of their guidance in his manner of writing, —though in this also I reckon he learned something from them, especially from the English Bible.

Besides the books which he read, he carried about with him little blank-books in which he jotted down the noteworthy in what he saw, heard, or imagined. He learned also from penless authors, composers without a manuscript, masters of the *viva-voce* style, like Robert, the Scotch gardener, and John Todd, the shepherd. When he saw a beggar on horseback, he cared not where the horse came from, he watched the rascal ride. If an expression struck him "for some conspicuous force, some happy distinction," he promptly annexed it;—because he understood it, it was his.

In two separate essays, each of which he calls

"A Gossip," he pays tribute to "the bracing influence of old Dumas," and to the sweeping power and broad charm of Walter Scott, "a great romantic—an idle child," the type of easy writers. But Stevenson is of a totally different type, though of a kindred spirit. He is the best example in modern English of a careful writer. He modelled and re-modelled, touched and retouched his work, toiled tremendously. The chapter on Honolulu in *The Wrecker*, was rewritten ten times. His essays for *Scribner's Magazine* passed through half a dozen revisions.

His end in view was to bring his language closer to life, not to use the common language of life. That, he maintained, was too diffuse, too indiscriminate. He wished to condense, to distil, to bring out the real vitality of language. He was like *Sentimental Tommy* in Barrie's book, willing to cogitate three hours to find the solitary word which would make the thing he had in mind stand out distinct and unmistakable. What matter if his delay to finish his paper lost him the prize in the competition? Tommy's prize was the word; when he had that his work was crowned.

A willingness to be content with the wrong colour, to put up with the word which does not fit, is the mark of inferior work. For example, the author of *Trilby*, wishing to describe a certain quick, retentive look, speaks of the painter's "*prehensile* eye." The adjective startles, but does not illuminate. The prehensile quality belongs to tails rather than to eyes.

There is a modern school of writers fondly given to the cross-breeding of adjectives and nouns. Their idea of a vivid style is satisfied by taking a subject which belongs to one region of life and describing it in terms drawn from another. Thus if they write of music, they use the language of painting; if of painting, they employ the terminology of music. They give us pink songs of love, purple roars of anger, and gray dirges of despair. Or they describe the andante passages of a landscape, and the minor key of a heroine's face.

This is the extravagance of a would-be pointed style which mistakes the incongruous for the brilliant. Stevenson may have had something to do with the effort to escape from the polished commonplace of an English which admitted no master earlier than Addison or later than Macaulay. He may have been a leader in the hunting of the unexpected, striking, pungent word. But for the excesses and absurdities of this school of writing in its decadence, he had no liking. He knew that if you are going to use striking words you must be all the more careful to make them hit the mark.

He sets forth his theory of style in the essay called *A Humble Remonstrance*. It amounts to this: First, you shall have an idea, a controlling thought; then you shall set your words and sentences marching after it as soldiers follow their captain; and if any turns back, looks the other way, fails to keep step, you shall put him out of the ranks as a malingerer, a deserter at heart. "The proper method of literature," says he, "is by selection, which is a kind of negative exaggeration." But the positive exaggeration,—the forced epithet, the violent phrase, the hysterical paragraph,—he does not allow. Hence we feel at once a restraint and an intensity, a poignancy and a delicacy in his style, which make it vivid without ever becoming insane even when he describes insanity, as he does in *The Merry Men*,

Olalla, and *Dr. Jekyll and Mr. Hyde.* His words are focussed on the object as with a burning-glass. They light it up; they kindle it; but they do not distort it.

Now a style like this may have its occasional fatigues: it may convey a sense of over-carefulness, of a choice somewhat too meticulous,—to use a word which in itself illustrates my meaning. But after all it has a certain charm, especially in these days of slipshod, straddling English. You like to see a man put his foot down in the right place, neither stumbling nor swaggering. The assurance with which he treads may be the result of forethought and concentration, but to you, reading, it gives a feeling of ease and confidence. You follow him with pleasure because he knows where he is going and has taken pains to study the best way of getting there.

Take a couple of illustrations from the early sketches which Stevenson wrote to accompany a book of etchings of Edinburgh,—hack work, you may call them; but even hack work can be done with a nice conscience.

Here is the Edinburgh climate: "The weather is raw and boisterous in winter, shifty and ungenial in summer, and a downright meteorological purgatory in spring. The delicate die early, and I, as a survivor among bleak winds and plumping rains, have been sometimes tempted to envy them their fate."

Here is the Scottish love of home: (One of the tall "lands," inhabited by a hundred families, has crumbled and gone down.) "How many people all over the world, in London, Canada, New Zealand, could say with truth, 'The house I was born in fell last night'!"

Now turn to a volume of short stories. Here is a Hebridean night, in *The Merry Men*: "Outside was a wonderful clear night of stars, with here and there a cloud still hanging, last stragglers of the tempest. It was near the top of the flood, and the Merry Men were roaring in the windless quiet."

Here is a sirocco in Spain: "It came out of malarious lowlands, and over several snowy sierras. The nerves of those on whom it blew were strung and jangled; their eyes smarted with the dust;

their legs ached under the burden of their body; and the touch of one hand upon another grew to be odious."

Now take an illustration from one of his very early essays, *Notes on the Movements of Young Children*, printed in 1874. Here are two very little girls learning to dance: "In these two, particularly, the rhythm was sometimes broken by an excess of energy, *as though the pleasure of the music in their light bodies could endure no longer the restraint of the regulated dance.*"

These examples are purposely chosen from tranquil pages; there is nothing far-fetched or extraordinary about them; yet I shall be sorry for you, reader, if you do not feel something rare and precious in a style like this, in which the object, however simple, is made alive with a touch, and stands before you as if you saw it for the first time.

II

Tusitala,—"Teller of Tales,"—was the name which the South Sea Islanders gave to Stevenson; and he liked it well. Beginning as an essayist, he turned more and more, as his life went on, to the art of prose fiction as that in which he most desired to excel. It was in this field, indeed, that he made his greatest advance. His later essays do not surpass his earlier ones as much as his later stories excel his first attempts.

Here I conceive my reader objecting: Did not *Treasure Island* strike twelve early in the day? Is it not the best book of its kind in English?

Yes, my fellow Stevensonian, it is all that you say, and more,—of its kind it has no superior, so far as I know, in any language. But the man who wrote it wrote also books of a better kind,—deeper, broader, more significant, and in writing these he showed, in spite of some relapses, a steadily growing power which promised to place him in the very highest rank of English novelists.

The Master of Ballantrae, maugre its defects of construction, has the inevitable atmosphere of fate, and the unforgettable figures of the two brothers, born rivals. The second part of *David Balfour* is not only a better romance, but also a better piece of character drawing, than the first part. *St. Ives,*

which was left unfinished, may have been little
more than a regular "sword-and-cloak" story, more
choicely written, perhaps, than is usual among the
followers of "old Dumas." But Stevenson's other
unfinished book, *Weir of Hermiston*, is the torso of
a mighty and memorable work of art. It has the
lines and the texture of something great.

Why, then, was it not finished? Ask Death.

Lorna Doone was written at forty-four years:
The Scarlet Letter at forty-six: *The Egoist* at fifty-
one: *Tess of the D'Urbervilles* at fifty-one. Stevenson died at forty-four. But considerations of what
he might have done, (and disputes about the in-
soluble question,) should not hinder us from ap-
praising his actual work as a teller of tales which
do not lose their interest nor their charm.

He had a theory of the art of narration which he
stated from time to time with considerable definite-
ness and inconsiderable variations. It is not ob-
ligatory to believe that his stories were written on
this theory. It is more likely that he did the work
first as he wanted to do it, and then, like a true
Scot, reasoned out an explanation of why he had

done it in just that way. But even so, his theory remains good as a comment on the things that he liked best in his own stories. Let us take it briefly.

His first point is that fiction does not, and can not, compete with real life. Life has a vastly more varied interest because it is more complex. Fiction must not try to reproduce this complexity literally, for that is manifestly impossible. What the novelist has to do is to turn deliberately the other way, and seek to hold you by simplifying and clarifying the material which life presents. He wins not by trying to tell you everything, but by telling you that which means most in the revelation of character and in the unfolding of the story. Of necessity he can deal only with a part of life, and that chiefly on the dramatic side, the dream side; for a life in which the ordinary, indispensable details of mere existence are omitted is, after all, more or less dream-like. Therefore, the story-teller must renounce the notion of making his story a literal transcript of even a single day of actual life, and concentrate his attention upon those things which seem to him the most real in life,—the things that count.

Now a man who takes this view of fiction, if he excels at all, will be sure to do so in the short story, a form in which the art of omission is at a high premium. Here, it seems to me, Stevenson is a master unsurpassed. *Will o' the Mill* is a perfect idyl; *Markheim*, a psychological tale in Hawthorne's manner; *Olalla*, a love-story of tragic beauty; and *Dr. Jekyll and Mr. Hyde*, in spite of its obvious moving-picture artifice, a parable of intense power.

Stevenson said to Graham Balfour: "There are three ways of writing a story. You may take a plot and fit characters to it, or you may take a character and choose incidents and situations to develop it, or lastly you may take a certain atmosphere and get actions and persons to express and realize it. I'll give you an example—*The Merry Men*. There I began with the feeling of one of those islands on the west coast of Scotland, and I gradually developed the feeling with which that coast affected me." This, probably, is somewhat the way in which Hawthorne wrote *The House of the Seven Gables;* yet I do not think that is one of his best romances, any more than I think *The Merry Men* one of Stevenson's best short stories. It is not memorable as a tale. Only the bits of description live. *The Treasure of Franchard*, light and airy as it is, has more of that kind of reality which Stevenson sought. Therefore it seems as if his third "way of writing a story" were not the best suited to his genius.

The second way,—that in which the plot links and unfolds the characters,—is the path on which he shows at his best. Here the gentleman adventurer was at ease from the moment he set forth on it. In *Treasure Island* he raised the dime novel to the level of a classic.

It has been charged against Stevenson's stories that there are no women in them. To this charge one might enter what the lawyers call a plea of "confession and avoidance." Even were it true, it would not necessarily be fatal. It may well be doubted whether that primitive factor which psychologists call "sex-interest" plays quite such a predominant, perpetual, and all-absorbing part in real life as that which neurotic writers assign to it in their books. But such a technical, (and it must be confessed, somewhat perilous,) defense is not needed. There are plenty of women in Stevenson's books,—quite as many, and quite as delightful and important as you will find in the ordinary run of life. Marjory in *Will o' the Mill* is more lovable than Will himself. Olalla is the true heroine of the story which bears her name. Catriona and Miss Grant, in the second part of *David Balfour*, are girls of whom it would be an honour to be enamoured; and I make no doubt that David, (like Stevenson) was hard put to it to choose between them. Uma, in *The Beach of Falesa*, is a lovely insulated Eve. The two Kirsties, in *Weir of Hermiston*, are creatures of intense and vivid womanhood. It would have been quite impossible for a writer who had such a mother as Stevenson's, such a friend of youth as Mrs. Sitwell, such a wife as Margaret Vandegrift, to ignore or slight the part which woman plays in human life. If he touches it with a certain respect and *pudor*, that also is in keeping with his character,— the velvet jacket again.

The second point in his theory of fiction is that in a well-told tale the threads of narrative should converge, now and then, in a scene which expresses, visibly and unforgettably, the very soul of the story.

He instances Robinson Crusoe finding the footprint on the beach, and the Pilgrim running from the City of Destruction with his fingers in his ears.

There are many of these flash-of-lightning scenes in Stevenson's stories. The duel in *The Master of Ballantrae* where the brothers face each other in the breathless winter midnight by the light of unwavering candles, and Mr. Henry cries to his tormentor, "I will give you every advantage, for I think you are about to die." The flight across the heather, in *Kidnapped*, when Davie lies down, forspent, and Alan Breck says, "Very well then, I'll carry ye"; whereupon Davie looks at the little man and springs up ashamed, crying "Lead on, I'll follow!" The moment in *Olalla* when the Englishman comes to the beautiful Spanish mistress of the house with his bleeding hand to be bound up, and she, catching it swiftly to her lips, bites it to the bone. The dead form of Israel Hands lying huddled together on the clean, bright sand at the bottom of the lagoon of *Treasure Island*. Such pictures imprint themselves on memory like seals.

The third point in Stevenson's theory is, that

details should be reduced to a minimum in number and raised to a maximum in significance. He wrote to Henry James, (and the address of the letter is amusing,) "How to escape from the besotting *particularity* of fiction? 'Roland approached the house; it had green doors and window blinds; and there was a scraper on the upper step.' To hell with Roland and the scraper!" Many a pious reader would say "thank you" for this accurate expression of his sentiments.

But when Stevenson sets a detail in a story you see at once that it cannot be spared. Will o' the Mill, throwing back his head and shouting aloud to the stars, seems to see "a momentary shock among them, and a diffusion of frosty light pass from one to another along the sky." When Markheim has killed the antiquarian and stands in the old curiosity shop, musing on the eternity of a moment's deed,—"first one and then another, with every variety of pace and voice,—one deep as the bell from a cathedral turret, another ringing on its treble notes the prelude of a waltz,—the clocks began to strike the hour of three in the afternoon."

Turning over the bit of paper on which "the black spot," the death-notice of the pirates, has been scrawled with charcoal, Jim Hawkins finds it has been cut from the last page of a Bible, and on the other side he reads part of a verse from the last chapter of the Revelation: *Without are dogs and murderers.*

There is no "besotting particularity" in such details as these. On the contrary they illustrate the classic conception of a work of art, in which every particular must be vitally connected with the general, and the perfection of the smallest part depends upon its relation to the perfect whole. Now this is precisely the quality, and the charm, of Stevenson's stories, short or long. He omits the non-essential, but his eye never misses the significant. He does not waste your time and his own in describing the coloured lights in the window of a chemist's shop where nothing is to happen, or the quaint costume of a disagreeable woman who has no real part in the story. That kind of realism, of local colour, does not interest him. But he is careful to let you know that Alan Breck wore a sword that was much too long for him; that Mr. Hyde was pale and dwarfish, gave an impression of deformity without any nameable malformation, and bore himself "with a sort of murderous mixture of timidity and boldness"; that John Silver could use his wooden leg as a terrible weapon; that the kitchen of the cottage on Aros was crammed with rare incongruous treasures from far away; and that on a certain cold sunny morning "the blackbirds sung exceeding sweet and loud about the House of Durisdeer, and there was a noise of the sea in all the chambers." Why these *trivia?* Why such an exact touch on these details? Because they count.

Yet Stevenson's tales and romances do not give— at least to me—the effect of over-elaboration, of strain, of conscious effort; there is nothing affected and therefore nothing tedious in them. They move; they carry you along with them; they are easy to read; one does not wish to lay them down and take a rest. There is artifice in them, of course, but it is a thoroughly natural artifice,—as natural as a clean voice and a clear enunciation are to a well-bred gentleman. He does not think about them;

he uses them in his habit as he lives. Tusitala enjoys his work as a teller of tales; he is at home in it. His manner is his own; it suits him; he wears it without fear or misgiving,—the velvet jacket again.

III

Of Stevenson as a moralist I hesitate to write because whatever is said on this point is almost certain to be misunderstood. On one side are the puritans who frown at a preacher in a velvet jacket; on the other side the pagans who scoff at an artist who cares for morals. Yet surely there is a way between the two extremes where an artist-man may follow his conscience with joy to deal justly, to love mercy, and to walk humbly with his God. And having caught sight of that path, though he may trace it but dimly and follow it stumbling, surely such a man may say to his fellows, "This is the good way; let us walk in it." Not one of the great writers who have used the English language, so far as I know, has finished his career without wishing to moralize, to teach something worth learning, to stand in the pulpit of experience and give an honest message to the world. Stevenson was no exception to this rule. He avowed the impulse frankly when he said to William Archer, "I would rise from the dead to preach."

In his stories we look in vain for "morals" in the narrow sense,—proverbs printed in italics and tagged on to the tale like imitation oranges tied to a Christmas tree. The teaching of his fiction is like that of life, diffused through the course of events and embodied in the development of characters. But as the story unfolds we are never in doubt as to the feelings of the narrator,—his pity for the unfortunate; his scorn for the mean, the selfish, the hypocritical; his admiration for the brave, the kind, the loyal and cheerful servants of duty. Never at his lightest and gayest does he make us think of life as a silly farce; nor at his sternest and saddest does he leave us disheartened, "having no hope and without God in the world." Behind the play there is a meaning, and beyond the conflict there is a victory, and underneath the uncertainties of doubt there is a foothold for faith.

COMPANIONABLE BOOKS

I like what Stevenson wrote to an old preacher, his father's friend. "Yes, my father was a 'distinctly religious man,' but not a pious. . . . His sentiments were tragic; he was a tragic thinker. Now granted that life is tragic to the marrow, it seems the proper service of religion to make us accept and serve in that tragedy, as officers in that other and comparable one of war. Service is the word, active service in the military sense; and the religious man—I beg pardon, the pious man—is he who has a military joy in duty,—not he who weeps over the wounded."

This is the point of view from which Stevenson writes as a novelist; you can feel it even in a romance as romantic as *Prince Otto ;* and in his essays, where he speaks directly and in the first person, this way of taking life as an adventure for the valourous and faithful comes out yet more distinctly. The grace and vigour of his diction, the pointed quality of his style, the wit of his comment on men and books, add to the persuasiveness of his teaching. I can see no reason why morality should be drab and dull. It was not so in Stevenson's character, nor is it so in his books. That is one reason why they are companionable.

"There is nothing in it [the world]," wrote he to a friend, "but the moral side—but the great battle and the breathing times with their refreshments. I see no more and no less. And if you look again, it is not ugly, and it is filled with promise."